IN THE
BEGINNING

IN THE BEGINNING

ARTHUR J. FERCH

REVIEW AND HERALD PUBLISHING ASSOCIATION
Washington, DC 20039-0555
Hagerstown, MD 21740

This book was
Edited by Gerald Wheeler
Designed by Richard Steadham
Cover photos by H. Armstrong Roberts, Inc.
Type set: 11/12 Zapf

PRINTED IN U.S.A.

Library of Congress Cataloging in Publication Data

Ferch, Arthur J., 1940-
  In the beginning.

  Bibliography: p.
  1. Bible. O.T. Genesis—Criticism, interpretation, etc. I. Title.
BS1235.2.F45   1985   222'.1106   85-1946
ISBN 0-8280-0282-7

To Carole

סעא אשה מצא חרט

He who finds a good wife finds happiness.
Proverbs 18:22

Contents

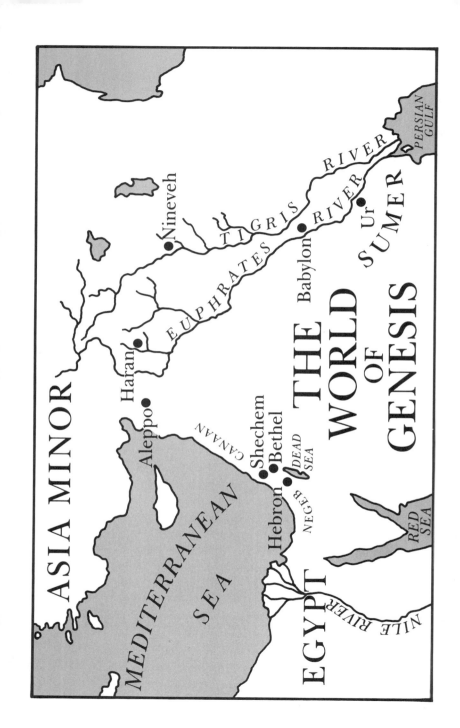

THE WORLD OF GENESIS

ASIA MINOR

MEDITERRANEAN SEA

EGYPT

NILE RIVER

RED SEA

Aleppo

Haran

Nineveh

EUPHRATES

TIGRIS RIVER

Babylon

Ur

SUMER

PERSIAN GULF

CANAAN

Shechem

Bethel

Hebron

DEAD SEA

NEGEB

Foreword

This book is a series of meditations on the first book of the Bible. Genesis travels a winding path from a glorious Creation to a closed coffin. It begins with fervent life, complete trust, and a sense of joyous fulfillment, and ends with tragic death, paralyzing suspicion, yet hopeful expectations of a better future. The universal breadth and fathomless depth of its themes and the poignant descriptions of its heroes have challenged human minds and hearts ever since Creation.

However, the path that begins with vibrant freedom is not to end with despondent bondage. Though the narrative comes to a conclusion, the book of Genesis is not an ending—it is merely a beginning. Through its promises of salvation, decendants, land, and expressions of future hope, the first book of Scripture points beyond itself to their consummation in the last book of the Bible.

The cataclysmic beginning of our world revealed in the book of Genesis *guarantees* the supernatural end of our planet when Eden lost will become Eden restored. A denial of the Biblical doctrine of Creation (protology) puts the scriptural teaching on the end (eschatology) in question. Eschatology cannot be without protology. Sabbath and Advent, memorials to both beginning and end, reveal not only God's sovereign work of grace but also the triumphant finale of the drama presently unfolding upon the stage of our history.

In the Beginning reflects the thought of a wide variety of authors, only few of whom I could directly acknowledge in the endnotes. Their thoughts and words provided both instruction and inspiration. Bible quotations generally come from *The New International Version* except those direct translations I have made myself.

I would like to express gratitude to the Avondale College Foundation for its generous research grant that made the final preparation of the manuscript possible. Thanks also go to Richard Coffen, book editor at the Review and Herald, for the invitation to write this volume.

Arthur J. Ferch ☐

The Book of Genesis

"There can scarcely be another part of Scripture over which so many battles, theological, scientific, historical, and literary, have been fought, or so many strong opinions cherished. This very fact is a sign of the greatness and power of the book, and of the narrow limits of both our factual knowledge and our spiritual grasp."[1] So wrote Derek Kidner in the preface of his short but comprehensive commentary on the book of Genesis.

Humanity has recognized the greatness and power of the first book of the Bible not only in the fact that it is authoritative Scripture but also in that it is a classic in human literature and the source of superbly executed works of art and music. Its sublime themes, stark realism, and transparent honesty distinguish it. Genesis brings its readers into the very presence of the Eternal and confronts them with questions of their origin, meaning in life, and destiny. Haydn's oratorio *The Creation* and Michelangelo's fresco *The Creation of Adam* in the Sistine Chapel trace their inspiration back to the first page of the Bible. Astronauts, circling the moon, read the first verses of Genesis.

The Sacred Word records as truthfully the jubilant pleasure of Adam over the first bride as it depicts the bitter pain that accompanied the sin of our first parents. Scripture registers both the successes and failures of its heroes. It is said that Oliver Cromwell instructed the painter of his portrait, "Paint me as I am, warts and all." So the book of Genesis records both the virtues and vices of Adam, Eve, Noah, Abraham, Sarah, Isaac, Jacob, and his family. No currently known document from the ancient Near East covers as broad a scope in time and subject as does Genesis.

The book acquired its name Genesis, meaning "origin" or "source," from the old Greek translation of the Old Testament known as the Septuagent. Like other documents of antiquity, the first book of the Hebrew Bible had as its title its opening phrase. The first word of Genesis, *bereshith*, means "in the beginning." *Bereshith* is the first of the five books that the Jews called Torah, i.e., "law," or better, "guidance." Greek-speaking Jews recognized this unit of five books and designated it by the adjective *pentateuchos* ("consisting of five scrolls") from which we derive the name Pentateuch. Later Bibles, beginning with Luther's translation and reflecting ancient Jewish tradition, entitled this book "The First Book of Moses [Commonly] Called Genesis" (e.g., the King James Version and the Revised Standard Version).

The book of Genesis divides naturally into two parts, the former listing three major events and the latter three major persons. The first section (chapters 1-11) deals with the earliest history of the world, and for this reason we designate it as primal, or primeval, history. The second part (chapters 12-50) is known as patriarchal history because it introduces us to the forefathers or patriarchs of the children of Israel. The three significant events in chapters 1-11 are (1) the Creation and Fall (chapters 1-4); (2) the Flood (chapters 6-9); and (3) the exodus of the ancestors of the Hebrew people from Ur (chapter 11). The three most important individuals featured in these events are Adam, Noah, and Abraham. Genealogies link the stories of the Creation and Fall, the Flood, and the patriarchal exodus. Thus chapter 5, which consists of a list of antedeluvian (i.e., pre-Flood) patriarchs, spans the period between the family of Adam and that of Noah. Similarly, chapter 10, a table of nations, and chapter 11, the genealogy of postdeluvian (i.e., post-Flood) patriarchs, connect Noah with Abraham. The genealogies, to which we will return in chapter 6, therefore act as bridges, as the following diagram illustrates:

GENESIS 1-11 PRIMEVAL HISTORY				
Creation and Fall (Chapters 1-4)	Genealogy bridging the gap between Adam and Noah (Chapter 5)	The Flood (Chapters 6-9)	Table of Nations (Chapter 10) Genealogy bridging the gap between Noah and Abraham	Exodus of patriarchal ancestors from Ur (Chapter 11)

Primeval history focuses on the world as a whole and on mankind in its entirety. We find phrases such as "the earth," "all living creature," et cetera. Thus Genesis 1:1 speaks of the creation of "the *heavens* and the *earth*." Similarly, Genesis 2:1 and 4 refer to the completion of "the *heavens* and the *earth*."

In the Flood account the Lord announced to Noah,

" 'I will wipe *mankind*, whom I have created, off from the face of the *earth*—men and animals, and creatures that move along the ground, and birds of the air' " (Gen. 6:7; compare chap. 7:21-23). After the Deluge God promised to remember the everlasting covenant between God " 'and all living creatures of *every* kind on the *earth*' " (chap. 9:16). The table of nations provides the names of those from whom "the nations spread out over the *earth* after the flood" (chap. 10:32). Before the destruction of the Tower of Babel "the *whole world* had one language and a common speech" (chap. 11:1).

In contrast to most of the Old Testament, which centers on Israel, the chosen people, and Palestine, their home, the worldwide context of Genesis 1-11 again appears in the prophecies of the book of Daniel (Dan. 2, 7-12), as well as in the universal mission of the Christian church announced in the New Testament. In the vision of the book of Daniel we break out of the narrow confines of Israel and Palestine and see the Babylonian, Medo-Persian, Greek, and succeeding empires within the plan and purpose of God. Both Jesus and Paul remind the Christian church to expand its mission from Jerusalem, Judea, and Samaria " 'to the ends of the earth' " (Acts 1:8; compare Col. 1:23).

This perspective of the primeval history gives a worldwide dimension to such divinely ordained institutions as the Sabbath and marriage (chap. 2:2, 3, 22-24). Likewise, the results of the fall and the divine promise (chapter 3) have universal dimensions. Given this global viewpoint, we would be unjustified to limit the Sabbath and the institution of marriage just to the later nation of Israel. Undoubtedly Jesus had this in mind when He stated, " 'The Sabbath was made for man' " (i.e., "mankind"; see Mark 2:27).

Turning to the patriarchal history, we notice three

prominent figures: Abraham (chaps. 11:26-25:8), Jacob (chap. 25:19-35:29; Genesis also mentions him in chapters 37 and 42-49), and Joseph, Jacob's favorite son (chaps. 37:1-50:26). The brief story of Isaac, Abraham's son of promise, appears between the narratives of Abraham and Jacob (see chaps. 21:1-28:9). The genealogy of Esau, Jacob's twin brother and ancestor of the Edomites, occurs between the Jacob and Joseph narratives (chapter 36). We may diagram this as follows:

GENESIS 12-50 PATRIARCHAL HISTORY				
Abraham (Chapters 11:26-25:8)	Isaac (Chapters 21:1-28:9)	Jacob (Chapters 25:19-35:29)	Genealogy of Esau (Chapter 36)	Joseph (Chapters 37-50

With the patriarchal history the author introduces us to the ancestors of the Hebrew nation. He narrows down his earlier global perspective to a particular family occupying a specific geographical region. In Genesis 12-50 Abraham and his descendants travel primarily in Palestine with occasional excursions into Egypt and one extended journey to Mesopotamia.

The genealogy of Shem (in chapter 11) has a double function. On the one hand, it interlocks the story of Abraham with that of the Creation-Fall-Flood account, and on the other, it links up with the following patriarchal stories, thus giving unity to the complete book.

However, the book of Genesis is not an island disconnected from the rest of Scripture. Several themes that begin here echo through the books of Exodus, Leviticus, Numbers, and Deuteronomy. Genesis is the foundation on which Exodus through Deuteronomy rest. Thus the genealogical line of the sons of Jacob (Gen. 46:8-27) surfaces again in Exodus 1:1-5. The blood relationship between Esau and Jacob provides the reason for God's command to bypass Edomite territory and not to provoke the Edomites to war as the Israelites moved toward the promised land (Deut. 2:4-8).

The ripples created by the themes of Genesis extend beyond the confines of the Pentateuch. The promise of descendants and land given to the childless and landless Abraham had only a partial fulfillment in Isaac and his descendants, the Israelites, at the time of the conquest of Palestine. Not until the time of David were these promises realized. And still, the writer to the Hebrews declares a millennium later, "All these people were still living by faith when they died. They did not receive the things promised. . . . They were longing for a better country—a heavenly one" (Heb. 11:13-16). Abraham was "looking forward to the city with foundations, whose architect and builder is God" (verse 10). Such passages suggest that the full consummation of the promises first given in Genesis will not occur until the new earth portrayed in the book of Revelation.

The first volume in Scripture is a book of Bible "firsts." Some of the ideas or actions first mentioned here include the use of sacrifices (Gen. 4:3, 4), a covenant between God and man (chap. 6:18), the distinction between "clean" and "unclean" animals (chap. 7:2), the principle of tithing (chap. 14:20), an oral vision (chap. 15:1), the phrase "the word of the Lord," which regularly introduces prophetic oracles (verse 1), the relationship between faith and righteousness (verse 6), the idea of a prophet (chap. 20:7), and the laying on of hands in blessing (chap. 48:14).

Since the book of Genesis adds no further information in the context of several of these Bible "firsts," one
may presuppose that the people had a knowledge of
their meaning and use. For example, Cain never
pleaded ignorance in regard to the sacrifice acceptable
in God's sight. Noah and his family raised no question
as to what constituted "clean" or "unclean" animals.
Since such questions posed no problem to either Cain
or Abel or Noah, we may assume an adequate
knowledge on their part of what constituted acceptable sacrifices or "clean" and "unclean" animals.
Instruction regarding such items at a much later
period in the books of Exodus, Leviticus, Numbers, and
Deuteronomy represented merely an expansion of
earlier knowledge.

As a seed contains the fruit, so the first book of the
Bible encompasses the origin of all the themes that
follow in Scripture. For this reason, our study of the
great subjects in Scripture must begin with their
source in Genesis.

The author of Genesis brings us face to face with
God. The book describes Him as the " 'Creator of
heaven and earth' " (chap. 14:19) and " 'Judge of all the
earth' " (chap. 18:25). The book applies a variety of
terms and names to Him. In speaking to the king of
Sodom, Abraham designated the Creator as " 'God
Most High' " (chap. 14:22). On several occasions God
revealed Himself to a patriarch who had succumbed to
human frailties and reassuringly identified Himself as
" 'God Almighty' " (chaps. 17:1; 35:11). Constantly aware
of the transitory nature of life, Abraham worshiped the
"Eternal God" (chap. 21:33).

Neither death nor the most powerful nations can
frustrate the plan and purpose that the God of Genesis

has for His children. We may entrust ourselves to the providential care of the Lord who led Abraham from Ur and permitted the tragedies in the life of Joseph to save both a young lad and his family (chap. 45:5-7). He who walked with Enoch (chap. 5:24) and sustained Jacob like a shepherd "all the days of his life" (chap. 48:15) is still trustworthy today. Eliezer praised the Lord who had " 'not abandoned his kindness and faithfulness' " to Abraham. He confessed, " 'As for me, the Lord has led me on the journey to the house of my master's relatives' " (chap. 24:27).

The book of Genesis affords us several intimate glimpses into God's heart. The narrator records the divine joy as God surveys His Creation (chap. 1:31) and sadly notes that "the Lord [employing human phraseology] was grieved that he had made man on the earth, and his heart was filled with pain" (chap. 6:6). But when Lot at the peril of his life hesitated to leave doomed Sodom, "the men grasped his hand and the hands of his wife and of his two daughters and led them safely out of the city, for the Lord was merciful to them" (chap. 19:16).

In this way Genesis depicts the God of power also as the God of love and compassion. The Creator Himself initiated the search for His straying children in the Garden of Eden. He provided them with the garments with which to cover their shame. The Lord placed a mark on Cain, the murderer, "so that no one who found him would kill him" (chap. 4:15). After Abram bargained over Sodom, the Lord responded, " 'for the sake of ten, I will not destroy it' " (chap. 18:32). When a substitute sacrifice took the place of his only son, Abraham memorialized Isaac's deliverance by naming the region of Moriah: " 'The Lord will provide' " (chap. 22:14).

Though sin now limited the possibilities with which God had endowed His first children, the book of Genesis assures its readers that nothing will frustrate the divine plan and purpose for humanity. Grace triumphs in the pages of the first book of the Bible. The translation of Enoch and the deliverance of Noah and his family guarantee the superabundance of grace. The experience of both Enoch and Noah illustrate the truthfulness of Paul's statement "Where sin increased, grace increased all the more" (Rom. 5:20). The sombre and death-drum-like beat of "and then he died" repeated through the genealogies suddenly halts at the startling comment "Enoch walked with God; then he was no more, because God took him away" (chap. 5:24).

Though death might reign for the moment, God's grace has robbed this enemy of supremacy. Genesis ends on a note of hope. Shortly before his death Joseph testified, " 'God will surely come to your aid and take you up out of this land to the land he promised on oath to Abraham, Isaac and Jacob. . . . God will surely come to your aid' " (chap. 50:24, 25). The journey that commenced with a vibrant Creation will not end with a coffin. Through its promises of salvation, seed, land, and blessing, the first book of the Bible points beyond itself. The prophets took up its strains and announced God's plan to create a " 'new heavens and a new earth,' " a promise that finds its consummation in the scenes painted by the book of Revelation (compare Isa. 65:17 and Rom. 8:18-25). It is precisely the beginning of our world depicted in the book of Genesis that guarantees the ultimate supernatural end when Eden lost will become Eden restored.

The Beginning of Life

The majestic account of Genesis 1 overpowers the sensitive reader like the roll of a cathedral organ. Stylistically it is both profound and simple and as such has the hallmarks of great literature. The chapter encompasses both "the heavens and the earth," yet at the same time it is also selective, for it does not lay claim to have mentioned everything we see around us.

The careful reader of Genesis 1 will detect in its poetic prose a magnificent architectural structure. Following the summary statement "In the beginning God created the heavens and the earth" and the introductory comment "Now the earth was formless and empty, darkness was over the surface of the deep, and the Spirit of God was hovering over the waters" are six structured stanzas (verses 3-5; 6-8; 9-13; 14-19; 20-23; 24-31).

The first three stanzas express the form that God gave to the "formless" earth, and the last three record how the Creator imparted fullness to its "emptiness." In this sense the first set of three (verses 3-13) complements the last set of three (verses 14-31). Thus the creation of light on the first day (verses 3-5) provided the day and the night. The elements of day and night were then complemented by the products of day four, namely the greater and the lesser luminaries, in the sense that the greater light would rule the day and the lesser light would govern the night. Accordingly, the Creator's activity of day four complements that of day one. Similarly, the action of day five complements day two. The skies above the firmament and the seas below, which God created on the second day, He filled by the creatures brought into existence on the fifth day. Likewise, the work of day six complements that of day three. The following diagram illustrates the pattern:

Introduction Verses 1 and 2

	Day	Greater light
Day 1: Light	Day 4	(verses 14-19)
(verses 3-5)	Night	Lesser Light
	Waters above	Birds
Day 2: Firmament	Day 5	(verses 20-23)
(verses 6-8)	Waters below	Fish
	Earth	Animals
Day 3: Division of land	Day 6	(verses 24-31)
and sea (verses	Plants	Man
9-13)		

Students of the Old Testament have also recognized a broad fivefold structure repeated throughout the stanzas. The five elements consist of:

1. An introduction: "God said."
2. A command: "Let there be."
3. The fulfillment: "It was so."
4. An evaluation: "God saw it was good."
5. A time element: "There was evening, and there was morning."

It becomes evident, then, that the Creation account presents its majestic themes with a literary beauty that befits the subject. The author's careful design, symmetry, and structure give evidence of his great literary skill. It depicts the totality of the world in all its dimensions of space and time. Spatially, the writer encompassed the whole creation in the introduction (verse 1) before he unfolded all its elements in the rest of the chapter (verses 21-31). Temporally, the author presented the creative acts in the time sequence of six days that reached its climax on the seventh day of God's rest.

The opening statement in the Bible is significant both for what it affirms and for what it denies. The words "In the beginning God created the heavens and the earth" clearly declare that the God of Creation is preexistent, sovereign, personal, beneficent, and that He provides purpose and meaning to all reality.

The narrative of Genesis 1 begins with God, continues with God, and ends with God. He is the subject of the first phrase ("in the beginning God"), and the word *God* introduces every subsequent paragraph. Finally, on the sixth day it is again God who beholds that which He has made and pronounces it "very good" (verse 31). Thirty-one verses mention the word *God* thirty-two times. God is before all, above all, and He is at the back of all.

Verse 1 assures the reader that God is uncreated and preexistent. Every creative act reminds us that God is before that which He brings into existence. The words "in the beginning God created" stress that He is before "time," while the phrase "God created the heavens and the earth" notes that He is also beyond "space."

However, the focus of Genesis 1 is not so much on God's preexistence as it is on His actions. Indeed, the activity of God is of greater importance to the Bible writers than His nature. We see this demonstrated in the use of action verbs like *separate, make, set, create, name, bless.* God *separated* the "light from the darkness" and the "water under the expanse from the water above it" (verses 4, 7). He *made* the "expanse" (verse 7), "two great lights" (verse 16), and "the wild animals (verse 25). The Creator *set* the "two great lights" in the "expanse of the sky to give light on the earth" (verses 16, 17). He *created* "the great creatures of the sea and every living and moving thing with which the water teems, according to their kinds, and every winged bird according to its kind" (verse 21). God *created* "man in his own image, in the image of God he created him; male and female he created them" (verse 27). The fact that God *named* the light "day," the darkness "night," the expanse "sky," the dry ground "land," and the waters "seas" (verses 5, 8, 10), and *blessed* our first parents (verses 27, 28), further stresses the divine activity.

The Creation account assures us that there is purpose and meaning in our world. God planned His creation and executed it according to His will. The words " '*Let* there be light' " (verse 3), " '*Let* there be an expanse' " (verse 6), " '*Let* the water under the sky be gathered to one place, and *let* dry ground appear' " (verse 9), " '*Let* the land produce vegetation' " (verse 11), " '*Let* there be lights in the expanse of the sky' " (verse 14), " '*Let* the water teem with living creatures, and *let* birds fly above the earth across the expanse of the sky' " (verse 20), " '*Let* the land produce living creatures' " (verse 24), and " '*Let* us make man in our image' " (verse 26) always precede the creative act. In this way the Bible stresses that creation originates in the will of God. In distinction from the pagan religions—as we will note later—Genesis 1 has nothing capricious, irrational, or erratic. The opening verse does not allow for mechanical chance or blind groping. Because heaven and earth began in the beneficent plan and purpose of God, we may rest assured that life has meaning. Life is more than merely "a tale told by an idiot, full of sound and fury, signifying nothing."[2]

God created the cosmos solely by His grace, and He rules it by His own inherent power. Like an undisputed sovereign, He transcends—is above and beyond—all creation. Because He is our Creator, He is also our Lord and is worthy to receive our worship, love, trust, and obedience. In sum, Genesis 1:1 affirms positively that God is personal, good, transcendent, preexistent, absolute, and omnipotent. All nature is subservient to Him whose will and purpose are unchallengeable.

However, the opening statement of Scripture is also important for what it implicitly denies. The phrase "in the beginning God created" clearly asserts the existence of God and therefore rules out the doctrine of atheism. Polytheism, with its notion of many gods, stands exposed, for Genesis confesses the *one* Creator. Our author further rejects materialism, which asserts the eternity of matter, for he boldly claims the *creation* of matter and asserts the existence of the spiritual in mankind. Since the first verse in the Bible assumes God's existence *before* and *beyond* Creation, it also distances itself from pantheism, which considers God and the universe to be identical. While the Biblical Creator may express Himself in terms of nature, He stands outside of and beyond nature, and therefore we must not confuse Him with the deity depicted by nature poets or nature mystics.

Scholars frequently pause in their examination of Genesis 1:1-3 to reflect on a comparison between the Biblical Creation story and Creation accounts found among other nations. In an analysis of the Creation stories from around the world, Claus Westermann notes four ways in which the theme of creation has been presented. First, there is *creation by means of generation*, as reflected in some Sumerian mythologies. In this grouping of stories the gods give birth to the elements. Second, one reads of *creation as a result of battle*, as classically reflected in the old Babylonian story entitled *Enuma Elish*. It reports the struggle between the gods Tiamat and Marduk in which the winner uses parts of the defeated saltwater deity Tiamat in the creative process. Third, we encounter *creation by means of forming or making*. A relief from Egypt, which depicts the god Khnum fashioning the prince Amenhotep III on a potter's wheel, illustrates this mode of creation. Finally, Westermann notes *creation by a word* and cites an example from the theology of ancient Memphis in Egypt.

Though the Bible accommodates itself to some of these images and occasionally even uses similar vocabulary, it remains distinct and unique within the ancient Near East. Studies that on a basis of similarity seek to demonstrate the dependence of the Bible on such traditions—especially the *Enuma Elish*—fail to recognize the even more important philosophical and theological distinctions that set the Biblical account off from the non-Biblical stories.

In contrast to the extra-Biblical Creation narratives from polytheistic religions, the Hebrew tradition of Creation rejects the idea of many gods. Whereas the God of Creation is uncreated, the gods—particularly in the *Enuma Elish*—came into existence by means of birth. Furthermore, they were indebted for their existence to some prior self-contained substance and therefore were limited in scope and power and lacked absolute freedom.

Wherever we observe a plurality of deities, we also find a multiplicity of ethical standards, moral values, and attributes. Invariably this has led to conflict. We find that although some of the gods insisted on acceptable conduct, ultimately they were all morally indifferent and capricious. The God of Genesis stands in contrast to them, for "morality and ethics constitute the very essence of His nature. The Bible presumes that God operates by an order which man can comprehend, and that a universal moral law has been decreed for society. Thus, the idea embedded in Genesis of one universal Creator has profound ethical implications. It means that the same universal sovereign will that brought the world into existence continues to exert itself thereafter making absolute, not relative, demands upon man, expressed in categorical imperatives— 'thou shalt,' 'thou shalt not.' "[3]

Again, the deities in the non-Hebrew mythologies were part of nature, a fact that had far-reaching implications for both the gods and those who worshiped them. Since the forces of nature appeared to be unpredictable and cruel, the people viewed their gods in the same way. The result was that worshipers in such a system had no feeling of certainty or security because everything appeared to be capricious. Also, such religions identified history and time with the cycle of nature. Since the seasons constantly repeat themselves, history became nothing more than a repetitive and unending cycle. Mankind found itself swept along mercilessly as by a tide, with no room for goals toward which humanity might strive.

On the contrary, Genesis 1 proclaims, as we have already indicated, that a single Mind is behind all that we see and feel. Reality has purpose and meaning.

Because life began in divine goodness, we may step out full of courage and joy and throw open our arms in expectation. The Word of God liberates its readers from the repressive and repetitive cycle of time inherent in the polytheism of Israel's neighbors, and opens the cycle into a line that has both a clear beginning and a clear end. Man created in the image and likeness of God is not a mere passive automaton manipulated by the gods, but a free moral agent invited to choose life within the protecting arms of a loving and personal God.

Genesis 1 heralds that which today's men and women need to hear. Instead of a feeling of insecurity, the God of Creation instills optimism; in place of a sense of futility, He assures us of our worth, importance, and significance. It comes as no surprise, then, to note that God's last message to a world that hurts because it has made Him merely one option among many begins with the words " 'Fear God and give him glory, because the hour of his judgment has come. Worship him who made the heavens, the earth, the sea and the springs of water' " (Rev. 14:7). In antiquity the presence of God or the gods was a given, whereas our present age considers the existence of God an option. What an indictment of our sophisticated age that the God-filled past should rebuke the Godless present.

Readers of the first three verses of Genesis in modern-language translations often find themselves puzzled by the fact that different Bible versions render the passage in a variety of ways. Thus the King James Version (K.J.V.) reads: "In the beginning God created the heaven and the earth. And the earth was without form, and void. . . . And God said, Let there be light: and there was light." The K.J.V. renders the original Hebrew by short sentences that are understood to mean that nothing of our planet existed prior to day one of Creation week.

On the other hand, *The New American Bible* (N.A.B.) reads: "In the beginning, when God created the heavens and earth, the earth was a formless wasteland. . . . Then God said, 'Let there be light,' and there was light.'" The N.A.B. treats the original Hebrew of verses 1 and 2 as one long sentence in which verse 2 reports the condition of our earth before day one of Creation. Accordingly, our planet was already in existence as an inert mass prior to the first day of Creation, though its elements still had not been formed into surface features.

Though stylistic considerations and the ancient translations of the book of Genesis favor the rendition of the K.J.V., the fact of the matter is that the original consonantal Hebrew of verses 1-3 may have either the meaning conveyed by the K.J.V. or the N.A.B., and we should avoid dogmatism. However, it in no wise justifies the notion that the inert mass of which our planet consists came into existence independent of God. The clear testimony of Genesis 1 and of the rest of Scripture is that *ultimately* only the God of Creation is uncreated, and everything else owes its existence to Him. This truth is nonnegotiable, as we have already discovered. "By faith we understand that the universe was formed at God's command, so that what is seen was not made out of what was visible" (Heb. 11:3).

While in regard to the precise time of the "beginning" of Genesis 1:1 we cannot share the confidence of Bishop John Lightfoot, vice-chancellor of Cambridge University, who suggested that God created Adam on October 23, 4004 B.C., at 9:00 A.M., forty-fifth meridian time, it is clear that the Bible intends us to recognize a short chronology rather than the millions of years proposed by biological evolution.

The particular form of the Hebrew word translated "to create" (*bara'*) in Genesis 1:1 Scripture uses only to describe creative acts of God. However, in Genesis 1 and 2 we find the verb "to create" paralleled by the companion words "to make" (chap. 2:3, 4), "to form" (chaps. 1:26, 27; 2:7), and "to build" (chap. 2:22), all three of which may imply the use of preexisting matter (e.g., verses 7, 19). Thus God created by means of a word of command (e.g., Ps. 33:9) or by the use of matter that He already had brought into existence.

Neither our inability to pinpoint the moment of Creation nor the fact that God used previously created matter in the formation of our earthly home undermines the convictions of Seventh-day Adventists that (1) our habitable globe came into existence over a period of six literal days; (2) ultimately God brought all things into existence by a creative act or acts; and (3) God was not indebted to preexisting matter, but created our world out of nothing.[4]

Twins of Eden

"When God made heaven and earth He built a cathedral of time and called it the Sabbath. He has invited us to enter this cathedral one day each week to receive rest, worship, and the sheer joy of his presence."— Niels-Erik Andreasen.

In the present arrangement of the Biblical text the institutions of the Sabbath and the home flank Genesis 2. Both have their source in the creation of the cosmic order and the sinless setting of the Garden of Eden.

The origin of the Sabbath has generated considerable debate among students of the Old Testament. Some have linked the Biblical Sabbath with a special day in Mesopotamia called *shapattu*. While the name is virtually identical with the Hebrew *shabbath* ("the sabbath") and the cuneiform texts describe the Mesopotamian day as the "day of the quieting of the heart," we have no evidence that the Babylonian *shapattu* was a day of cessation from work for most people.

Moreover, the Babylonians regarded the seventh, fourteenth, twenty-first, and twenty-eighth day of certain months in their lunar calendar as "unlucky" or "evil" days. On these days, corresponding to the four phases of the moon, the physician, oracular priest, and especially the king were prevented from functioning in any official or professional capacity. However, there seems to be no link between such "evil days," thought to be controlled by evil spirits, and the day called *shapattu*. Nor do we have any evidence that the four "seventh days" provided rest for any except certain specific classes of people.

The Biblical Sabbath was very different from the Mesopotamian days. Though Genesis 2:2, 3 avoids the nominal form *shabbath* ("sabbath") and makes no reference to a fixed institution, its use of the verb *shabat* ("to cease," "abstain from labor") and the threefold reference to "the seventh day" link the seventh day of Creation week with the weekly day of rest described elsewhere in Scripture. By stating that God rested on the seventh day, that He blessed it and made it holy, the Bible writer divorced it from any links with the phases of the moon and stressed that the day derived its unique spiritual character from God alone. The late Jewish scholar Nahum Sarna emphasized this fact when he stated, "The seventh day is what it is, because God chose to 'bless it and declared it holy.' Its blessed and sacred character is part of the divinely ordained cosmic order. It cannot, therefore, be abrogated by man, and its sanctity is a reality irrespective of human activity."[5]

According to Genesis 2: 2, 3 we find the origin of the Sabbath and the weekly cycle in God's rest on the seventh day of Creation week. It is His rest that provides the reason for our rest. Exodus 20:8 and 11 state the same concept: "Remember the Sabbath day by keeping it holy. . . . For in six days the Lord made the heavens and the earth, the sea, and all that is in them, but he rested on the seventh day. Therefore the Lord blessed the Sabbath day and made it holy." Similarly, Exodus 31:12-17 understood the rest of God as the source for the weekly day of rest. " 'The Israelites are to observe the Sabbath, celebrating it for the generations to come as a lasting covenant. It will be a sign between me and the Israelites forever, for in six days the Lord made the heavens and the earth, and on the seventh day he abstained from work and rested' " (verses 16, 17). Genesis 2:2, 3 is the only Biblical source that recites the founding of the weekly Sabbath day.

Both the narratives and legislation contained in the rest of the Pentateuch presuppose the existence of the Sabbath. Well before the Israelites reached Mount Sinai, where He gave them the Decalogue, God tested them in regard to the Sabbath. In "the Desert of Sin, which is between Elim and Sinai" (Ex. 16:1), God supplied the hungry and grumbling community of Israelites with manna. He instructed Moses, " 'On the sixth day they are to prepare what they bring in, and that is to be twice as much as they gather on the other days' " (chap. 16:5). On the sixth day Moses commanded the Israelites: " ' "Tomorrow is to be a day of rest, a holy Sabbath to the Lord. So bake what you want to bake and boil what you want to boil. Save whatever is left and keep it until morning" ' " (verse 23). Since some of the people went out on the Sabbath despite clear instructions to the contrary, Moses reproved them with the words " 'How long will you refuse to keep my commands and my instructions? Bear in mind that the Lord has given you the Sabbath' " (verses 28, 29). Though this is the first time the Bible specifically mentions the weekly day of rest by name, the story clearly presupposes the Sabbath as a known institution, for we have no hint of its being instituted on that occasion. Rather, it appears to have been well-known already, a conclusion further supported by the words "*remember* the Sabbath day" and "*observe* the Sabbath day" in the fourth commandment in both versions of the Decalogue (Ex. 20:8 and Deut. 5:12). The command to "remember" implies that the Israelites were well acquainted with the Sabbath as the divinely ordained day of rest.

Since the rest instituted by God on the seventh day was part of the creation of the world, the book of Genesis gives the ordinance of the Sabbath—modeled on God's own example during the Creation week—universal validity. Adam and Eve and their children, whether literal or spiritual Israel, were invited to celebrate the Sabbath. We cannot limit the enjoyment of the weekly day of rest to the Jews, for it existed long before the formation of the Jewish community. Because the Sabbath was woven into the very warp and woof of our world, we have to recognize the universal dimensions of God's rest day. The seventh day of the week is the only day on which the Creator Himself rested and the only day that He blessed and set apart for a holy use.

By bestowing His blessing on the Sabbath, God endowed it with happiness. The Sabbath is to be beneficial to man. Thus the Hebrew Sabbath is the very antithesis of the evil days of Mesopotamia. "On the Sabbath day," Niels-Erik Andreasen notes, "masters have no servants and servants have no masters. It is a day of equality and freedom—not only freedom from work, but also freedom for God." Moreover, to sanctify the seventh day meant to separate it exclusively for God. The Sabbath affords us opportunity for worship, instruction, and meditation upon the Creator. With Adam and Eve we may be guests at God's Sabbath and partake of its joy and rest.

The combination of the universality and blessedness of the Sabbath carried with it social implications.

After the Exodus from Egypt the Lord spelled them out more fully when He asked the Israelites to " 'remember that you were slaves in Egypt and that the Lord your God brought you out of there with a mighty hand and an outstretched arm. Therefore the Lord your God has commanded you to observe the Sabbath day' " (Deut. 5:15).

Their experience in and deliverance from Egypt provided an additional reason for the need of the refreshment that the Sabbath could offer to body and soul. Nobody was to be excluded from this rest, whether young or old, male or female, free or slave, alien or resident—not even the animals (Ex. 20:10; 23:12).

Tragically, the *form* of the Sabbath soon eclipsed the *spirit* of the day of rest. The wholesome injunction prohibiting ordinary labor on the Sabbath designed to provide rest and joy became in the hands of some a distorted, unbending, harsh, and even unreasoned command. The regulations curtailing physical effort on the Sabbath became exaggerated to such a degree that in the time of Christ rabbis debated whether a legless man could go out on the Sabbath with his wooden stump without transgressing the law. All agreed that in case of an outbreak of fire one could suspend the command against carrying burdens on the Sabbath.[6]

Jesus repeatedly found Himself involved in disputes with the rabbis over proper Sabbath observance. On several occasions He reasoned that if they made their own exceptions to Sabbath regulations in lesser matters, He should be allowed to carry on His own work in the greater matters. For example, someone's aiding an animal that had fallen into a pit "broke" the Sabbath (Matt. 12:11). In the light of this Jesus argued, " 'How much more valuable is a man than a sheep!

Therefore it is lawful to do good on the Sabbath' " (verse 12; compare Luke 13:15, 16; John 7:22, 23). In this way Jesus demonstrated that His work of healing was the fulfillment of the redemptive intent of the Law. *Instead of abolishing the form of the Sabbath, Jesus*, the Creator made flesh, *sought to restore its spirit*. His life, words, and works rebuke those who use the excesses associated with the form of the Sabbath as a pretext for disobedience or repudiation of the sacred day of rest.

The days of Creation week have their goal in a day that was different from the rest. The work of Creation, which began with the separation of light from darkness, climaxed in the division of time into secular days and sacred days. Thus ordinary days flowed into a special day. Nowadays we cannot forget that "the work which has been laid upon man is not his goal. His goal is the eternal rest which has been suggested in the rest of the seventh day."[7]

As the Sabbath introduced the context of Genesis 2, so the institution of the home concludes the chapter. The first home was constituted by Adam and Eve, whom God in His sovereign grace chose from among the vast creation as His counterparts with whom to commune

The creation of our first parents differed significantly from the rest of the created orders. God called human beings into existence not by a divine command, but by the solemn announcement " 'Let us make man in our image, in our likeness, and let them rule over the fish of the sea and the birds of the air, over the livestock, over all the earth, and over all the creatures that move along the ground' " (Gen. 1:26). This divine resolution, varying from the previous formula of command "Let there be" that preceded the acts of Creation (see verses 3, 6, 9, 11), suggests that the position of mankind is unique within Creation.

God established a special relationship with Adam and Eve by creating them "in his own image, in the image of God he created . . . them" (verse 27). The same passage indicates that "man" created in God's image consists of both "male" and "female." It takes two different sexes to express what Scripture means by "human." Paul returns to this definition of humanity when he affirms the spiritual equality of the sexes in the celebrated verse "There is neither Jew nor Greek, slave nor free, male nor female, for you are all one in Christ Jesus" (Gal. 3:28). Similarly, Peter admonishes husbands to treat their wives with respect and as "heirs with you of the gracious gift of life" (1 Peter 3:7).

The meaning of the phrase " 'in our image, in our likeness' " has been the subject of vigorous and seemingly endless debates. However, before we make any decision as to what it stands for, we should remember two significant points. First, Genesis 1:26 does not place the conjunction *and* between "image" and "likeness." The text simply reads "in our image, in our likeness," indicating that the words "image" and "likeness" duplicate each other. Second, Genesis 5:1 and 3 essentially parallel Genesis 1:26, 27. Just as Adam and Eve were created in the likeness of God, so Scripture declares that Seth, Adam's son, is in the "likeness" and in the "image" of his father. It suggests that those interpretations that contend that God's image consists of the spirit or intellect in man fall short of the Biblical intention. In some mysterious sense man in his totality is a "transcription of the eternal incorporeal creator in terms of temporal, bodily, creaturely existence—as one might attempt a transcription of, say an epic into a sculpture, or a symphony into a sonnet." [8] Westermann adds correctly that "man, in his entirety, corporeally as well as spiritually and intellectually, is to be designated as a creature in God's image."[9] It is noteworthy that even after the entry of sin, Scripture declares mankind still to be in the image of God (see Gen. 9:6 and James 3:9).

Occasionally the Bible may, for the sake of convenience, analyze human beings into two or more constituents (e.g., 1 Thess. 5:23), but its central thrust is always to describe a person as a unit. The complement to Genesis 1:26, 27 is chapter 2:7: "The Lord God formed man from the dust of the ground and breathed into his nostrils the breath of life, and *man became a living being.*" We should not be confused by the translation in the K.J.V. of the Herew word *nephesh* by "soul." Such a rendering—avoided by the more modern versions— has led readers to think of the immortality of the soul. The latter notion "is not a Hebrew but a Greek idea. In Hebrew the 'soul' is not a part of 'man' but the whole living person, consisting, as this verse makes clear, of his body plus the breath which gives it life. . . . How different all this is from the Greek view that a person's material body may perish but that his or her 'soul' will live forever! That view only became familiar to Judaism and Christianity when in later centuries they moved into the Greek-speaking world, and it has caused untold theological damage ever since."[10] The Bible neither divides mankind into "flesh" and "spirit," nor does it tolerate the undervaluing of the flesh and the overvaluing of the spirit.[11] The Scriptures depict human beings wholistically, including their physical, moral, and intellectual life.

Genesis declares that the human family has links with both the ground and with God. Though He formed man of the dust, God created him in the divine image and gave him His animating breath. He who kissed us into existence assures us that He is intimately close to us and that we belong to Him. Regardless of sex or race, we are infinitely precious. By virtue of creation God bestowed an *inalienable* dignity upon every human being.

To be in the "image of God" also entails responsibility and accountability. As a consequence of the divine image, our first parents were to care for their environment. This accountability made possible the questions " 'Where are you?' " and " 'Have you eaten from the tree that I commanded you not to eat from?' " (chap. 3:9, 11).

God placed Adam and Eve in a garden of vegetation both attractive to the palate and sight and ample for nourishment. Like a father, He surrounded His children with arms of love and provided opportunities for their physical, intellectual, moral, and aesthetic growth. No better model for the home has been provided than that which God established and modeled in Eden.

In such a setting the Creator officiated at the first marriage. With a jubilant shout expressed in poetic verse Adam welcomed his bride: " 'This is now bone of my bones and flesh of my flesh; she shall be called "woman," for she was taken out of man' " (chap. 2:23). Marriages, established in the context of the dignity, equality, and responsibility that creation in the image of God bestows upon mankind, provide a companionship in which both partners give and take and thus promote their individual and mutual growth and unity. Such a union enables the couple to rise above selfishness and purify the affections.

The book of Genesis endows conception and matrimony with sacredness. In the words " 'Be fruitful and increase in number; fill the earth and subdue it' " (chap. 1:28) God blessed procreation and lifted it above blind instinct. Similarly, the writer of Genesis affirms, "For this reason a man will leave his father and mother and be united to his wife, and they will become one flesh" (chap. 2:24).

Legitimate sexual love does not embarrass the Bible. We should not confuse lawful sex with the sins of the flesh, nor should we identify holiness with asceticism. The Song of Solomon celebrates such affection and sexual love, and the book of Hebrews endorses the fact that "marriage should be honored by all, and the marriage bed kept pure, for God will judge the adulterer and all the sexually immoral" (Heb. 13:4).

The Sabbath and the home testify to our bond with both the Creator and the human race. Both institutions are gifts to us and lay claims upon us. In a sense the Sabbath and the home epitomize our duty to God and man and are therefore appropriately placed at the heart of the Decalogue (Ex. 20:8-12). Indeed, these twins in Eden provide the grounds for the two greatest commandments, "love of God" and "love of our neighbor," on which hang all the law and the prophets (Matt. 22:36-40). Wherever "love of God" and "love of neighbor" reign supreme, men and women may have a foretaste of Eden restored.

Lost and Found

"They hand in hand with wandering steps and slow,
Through *Eden* took their solitarie way."—J. Milton,
Paradise Lost, Book XII.

A new figure that now entered human history
shattered the peace and harmony that had characterized the Garden of Eden. It introduced untold sorrow,
misery, hatred, and death. This new being used a
serpent as its tool, as we may infer from God's curse
upon the serpent: " 'I will put enmity between you and
the woman, and between your offspring and hers; he
will crush your head, and you will strike his heel' "
(Gen. 3:15). The real identity behind the serpent Paul
unveils in his allusion to this verse: "The God of peace
will soon crush *Satan* under your feet" (Rom. 16:20).
Jesus condemned the same agent as a liar and
" 'murderer from the beginning' " (John 8:44).

Cunningly the tempter avoided any debate with
Eve. Instead he approached her with a question
expressed in an incredulous tone: " 'Did God *really* say
. . . ?' " He then added an exaggeration: "You must not
eat from *any* tree in the garden?" (Gen. 3:1). The serpent
misrepresented the divine instruction, for God had
never prohibited their access to *all* trees in the garden.
The words of the Lord to Adam were " 'You are free to
eat from any tree in the garden; but you must not eat

from the tree of the knowledge of good and evil, for when you eat of it you will surely die' " (chap. 2:16, 17). The exaggeration distorted God's instruction and caricatured His character, imputing harshness and injustice to Him. In this way Satan confused the issue.

God set before Adam and Eve the serious matter of obedience and allowed them to make a decision. The guidelines given by their divine Father were few, succinct, and clear. The command—as every other divine instruction—arose from love, and through it one could hear the love of the speaker. Like a caring parent, the Lord wanted His children to enjoy happiness, life, and joy, but He left the choice between life and death to them. His command in Eden demonstrates that He created all of us as free and responsible beings. Further, God's instruction reveals that evil was not a principle inherent in the world, but is the product of human choices and behavior. The fact that "God saw all that he had made, and it was very good" rules out the idea that something in Creation was responsible for the wrong choices of our first parents.

Eve's response to the tempter is significant. The Creator's words had been unmistakable and emphatic: " 'When you eat of it [i.e., from the tree of the knowledge of good and evil] you will surely die' " (verse 17). Yet in the original Hebrew, her reply to the serpent seems to indicate that she had modified God's threat. Instead of repeating the certainty with which God had stated the death penalty, her response implied that death was merely a possible event (chap. 3:3). She did not take God seriously, and by reflecting the doubt and hesitancy of the serpent, Eve played into Satan's hands. The belief that God loved the human pair too much to execute the sentence that He had pronounced may have generated her doubts.

From exaggeration and caricature the tempter now moved to open denial. First Satan had merely questioned God's stipulation. Now he contradicted the Lord as dogmatically as God had been emphatic in His declaration of the penalty. Defiantly, the serpent claimed, "Most certainly you will not die" (see verse 4). Moreover, Satan tempted Adam and Eve to distrust God's love and to doubt His wisdom (verse 5).

The promise that their eyes would be opened implied that they could overcome their current limitations of sight should they follow Satan's suggestion to disobey God's explicit command. No longer were the human pair content to be in the "image of God." Rather, they desired to be equal with Him. Thus they would no longer regard Him as sovereign and friend, but as a rival enemy.

The tempter "insinuated that the Lord jealously desired to withhold it [i.e., the forbidden fruit] from them, lest they should be exalted to equality with Himself. It was because of its wonderful properties, imparting wisdom and power, that He had prohibited them from tasting or even touching it. The tempter intimated that the divine warning was not to be actually fulfilled; it was designed merely to intimidate them. How could it be possible for them to die? Had they not eaten of the tree of life? God had been seeking to prevent them from reaching a nobler development and finding greater happiness." [12]

Ever since Eve's fateful decision to leave the security that Providence had offered, men and women have been tempted to believe that freedom from God and His will provides them with greater liberties and opens up broader fields of knowledge. Such a denial of God's sovereignty has always gone hand in hand with the rejection of the doctrine of the judgment. With

adolescent vehemence men and women proclaim
their independence and arrogantly assert their self-
sufficiency. Such an attitude the words of the British
critic and dramatist William Ernest Henley well
express:

> "It matters not how strait the gate,
> How charged with punishments the scroll,
> I am the master of my fate:
> I am the captain of my soul."

—Invictus

Relying on the promise of the creature rather than
trusting the word of the Creator, Eve decided to
disbelieve God's love and to question His wisdom.
Standing only in her own strength, she surrendered to
the temptation. The ingredients of sin still consist of
doubt in God's love and wisdom, of trust in the
creature rather than in the Creator, and of reliance on
the impressions of our senses. Once she had trans-
gressed, she became Satan's agent to bring about the
ruin of her husband (compare 1 Tim. 2:14).

God still appeals to our love and reminds us that we
can find life only in trust and obedience. In speaking to
the people of Israel, the Lord said, "Man does not live
on bread alone but on every word that comes from the
mouth of the Lord" (Deut. 8:3). He invites us to "taste
and see that the Lord is good; blessed is the man who
takes refuge in him" (Ps. 34:8).

In response to God's call " 'Where are you?' " Adam
replied, " 'I heard you in the garden, and I was afraid' "
(Gen. 3:10). It is the first expression of fear in the Bible
and was the natural result of the breach of love and
trust. This attitude has remained with all who are out
of harmony with God until they learn again that only
"perfect love drives out fear" (1 John 4:18). Tragically,
Adam and Eve had been "sold a false idea of evil, as

something beyond good; of wisdom, as sophistication; and now of greatness, as greed."[13] The consciousness of guilt spoiled their vision, and with the recognition of their own nakedness, fear seized the first human pair.

Adam claimed, " 'I was afraid because I was naked; so I hid' " (Gen. 3:10). He sought to hide the cause of his embarrassment, which was his disobedience, behind the symptoms of his sin, namely, his feeling of nakedness. Ever since, fallen beings have confused sin with its results and have mourned the punishment more than its cause. However, the Lord passed by the symptoms and focused on the real problem when He asked, " 'Have you eaten from the tree that I commanded you not to eat from?' " (verse 11). Before Adam could bring himself to confess, "I ate," he blamed his wife and in a sense accused God of being guilty for his fall. It was " 'the woman *you* put here with me—*she* gave me some fruit from the tree' " (verse 12). Adam shifted the responsibility from himself to God for giving him such a seductive partner. Similarly Eve, when challenged and questioned by God, charged the serpent with culpability for her guilt before admitting to her sin (verse 13).

The curse of sin fell not only upon the human couple but also upon the animal world and the environment. Millennia later, Paul noted that "the creation waits in eager expectation for the sons of God to be revealed. For the creation was subjected to frustration, not by its own choice, but by the will of the one who subjected it, in hope that the creation itself will be liberated from its bondage to decay and brought into the glorious freedom of the children of God. We know that the whole creation has been groaning as in the pains of childbirth right up to the present time" (Rom. 8:19-22). As the first pair "witnessed in drooping flower and falling leaf the first signs of decay, Adam and his companion mourned more deeply than men now mourn over their dead. The death of the frail, delicate flowers was indeed a cause of sorrow; but when the goodly trees cast off their leaves, the scene brought vividly to mind the stern fact that death is the portion of every living thing."[14]

The story of the Fall recorded here has left its impact upon the rest of Scripture and particularly upon the thought of Christianity. While the Old Testament testifies to man's bondage to sin, it makes little reference to the narrative in Genesis 3. However, Paul focused on this story and argued that "just as sin entered the world through one man, and death through sin, . . . in this way death came to all men, because all sinned" (chap. 5:12). Judaism, on the other hand, rejects the implications of the story of the Fall. According to Rabbi Isidore Epstein, the notion that Adam's sin "brought death upon all mankind is not alien to Judaism, but the reference is to physical death and is not to be confused with the doctrine of original sin involving the condemnation of the whole race to a death that is eternal and from which salvation can come only through a risen Saviour—a doctrine that has found no voice in the synagogue."[15]

To the Christian the full extent of Adam's fall becomes apparent only in the light of the accomplishments of the last Adam. The New Testament declares that as a result of sin mankind is as helpless as are homeless orphans, penniless debtors, condemned criminals, or helpless slaves. We can do nothing to restore ourselves to God or to improve our nature. But the good news is that God has taken the initiative to save us in Jesus Christ. He freely provides us with a home, eliminates our debts, justifies and reconciles us to Himself, and redeems us from our bondage. Through the work of Jesus Christ "the great dragon was hurled down—that ancient serpent called the devil or Satan, who leads the whole world astray" (Rev. 12:9). Christ shared our humanity "so that by his death he might destroy him who holds the power of death—that is, the devil" (Heb. 2:14). It is a victory anticipated in words that have been described as the first gospel *(protevangelium)* in Scripture: " 'And I will put enmity between you and the woman, and between your offspring and hers; he will crush your head, and you will strike his heel' " (Gen. 3:15).

Following the expression of promise and hope contained in verse 15, God informed Adam and Eve of the tragic results of their sin. That which was to provide Eve with joy and fulfillment—namely, her relationship to both husband and children—would now be marred. Childbearing would acquire pain, and the equality between husband and wife announced in Eden would become subverted (see verse 16). Work, which God had given as a blessing, would now be threatened with failure. No longer would the soil yield nourishment spontaneously or abundantly. Humanity would have to extract food through anguish and toil (see verses 17-19). The curse made the tasks that belonged to the roles in the life of our parents both difficult and painful—and all because Adam had put Eve's word above that of God (see verse 17).

Genesis 3 demonstrates a correspondence between sin and punishment. The judgments pronounced by God fit the crime. He addressed the offenders in the order of their offenses. First the serpent (verses 14, 15), next Eve (verse 16), and finally Adam (verses 17-19). The food that the human couple had considered pleasant and desirable before the Fall now became unpleasant and difficult to obtain. The serpent was to "eat dust all the days" of its life, and Adam and Eve would consume their nourishment as a result of toil. Whereas friendly relationships had existed between Eve and the serpent prior to the Fall, subsequent to her disobedience hostilities would exist between the two. In a deeper sense, the enmity that God put between the human pair and the serpent was, in itself, an act of grace by which God enabled mankind to resist the evil one. In short, the first pair, which in its rebellion had sought to become independent of God, was punished by being made independent of God.[16]

Nevertheless, Adam and Eve did not succumb to despair. It is apparent from the play on Hebrew words for "Eve" *(chawwah)* and "life" *(chayyah)* that Adam had grasped the divine promise of descendants enunciated in verse 15. By faith he anticipated the promise of salvation and named his wife "mother of the living" rather than "mother of the doomed."

Although living under the curse, the first pair felt encouraged, as God provided them with coats of skin (verse 21). Though the garments were designed primarily to protect them from the elements, the death of the innocent victim must have set in motion a train of thought concerning God's provisions for their spiritual welfare also. As Adam and Eve and their children engaged in the sacrificial ritual the significance of God's grace and care for their spiritual well-being became even more apparent.

However, love is genuine only when it respects both mercy and justice. As a result of their disobedience God had to banish Adam and Eve from the garden (verse 23). They had to leave their familiar surroundings and step into the unknown, comforted only by the divine promise and expression of hope. Yet even their expulsion manifested both mercy and justice. On the one hand, their eviction preserved them from becoming immortal sinners, while on the other hand, it demonstrated God's extreme displeasure with sin.

The conflict between good and evil that rages in the human heart we may trace right back to the experience of Adam and Eve in Eden. Here we find the first flight of man away from God. After their sin "the man and his wife heard the sound of the Lord God as he was walking in the garden in the cool of the day, and they *hid* from the Lord God among the trees of the garden" (chap. 3:8). In the assurance that God would put enmity between the serpent and the woman we also find the first indication that the human heart would experience a *battle with evil* (see verse 15). Thus Genesis 3 explains the origin of the simultaneous attraction and repulsion to God and sin that we find in our lives. Paul expressed our ambivalence and conflict by observing: "In my inner being I delight in God's law; but I see another law at work in the members of my body, waging war agains the law of my mind and making me a prisoner of the law of sin at work within my members" (Rom. 7:22, 23).

However, Paul does not give in to despair. He expresses the conviction that because of Christ's life, death, and resurrection, sin—though still present in this age—need no longer exert dominion over us. For the believer the cross has broken the power of sin as an operating principle in his life. The apostle declares, "For we know that our old self was crucified with him so that the body of sin might be rendered powerless, that we should no longer be slaves to sin—because anyone who has died has been freed from sin." "*Therefore* do not let sin *reign* in your mortal body so that you obey its evil desires. . . . For *sin shall not be your master*, because you are not under law, but under grace" (Rom. 6:6, 7, 12-14). The New Testament ends with the assurance that the serpent's head will be crushed. At that time not only the *power* of sin will be broken but its very *presence* will be abolished (compare Rev. 21:4).

Meanwhile Adam and Eve had to witness the sad consequences of their sin. The tragic sequel to their disobedience illustrates rather poignantly the principle that "a man reaps what he sows" (Gal. 6:7). Sin did not deteriorate humanity gradually—mankind quickly plunged to greater depths. Fratricide soon followed disobedience. Cain gave no evidence of remorse or confession for the murder of his brother. God's question "'Where is your brother?'" went unanswered. The firstborn of the race preferred exile from God to fellowship with Him. The human response clearly limited divine mercy. Kidner comments that "while Eve had been talked into her sin, Cain will not even have God talk him out of it; nor will he confess to it, nor yet accept his punishment."[17]

Similarly, Lamech, Cain's descendant, not only prided himself on callously disposing of a lad for a mere wound but actually celebrated his murder with a song (chap. 4:23, 24). A wrong relationship to God revealed itself in a wrong relationship to one's fellow human beings. Human brotherhood had been shattered. From now on, mankind divided into the descendants of Cain and the descendants of Seth— worshipers at two different altars.

The Deluge

The story of the Flood occupies a central place between the account of Creation and the patriarchal narratives. It closes one era and opens another. The writer of Genesis conveys the centrality of the Deluge account by noting that numerically, Noah's generation was midway between Adam's and Abraham's (Gen. 5:3-32 and 11:10-26).

The link between the Flood story and the accounts of the Creation and the patriarchs we see further highlighted by the fact that elements of the genealogies of Noah surround the Flood story like an envelope. At least four individual components make up the genealogical pattern evident in Genesis 5. They are:

1. A lived x years (e.g., "When Seth had lived 105 years" [Gen. 5:6]).

2. A became father of B (e.g., "he became the father of Enosh" [verse 6]).

3. After A became the father of B, A lived x years and had other children (e.g., "And after he became the father of Enosh, Seth lived 807 years and had other sons and daughters" [verse 7]).

4. Altogether, A lived x years, and then he died (e.g., "Altogether, Seth lived 912 years, and then he died" [verse 8]).

In the case of Noah the story of the Flood breaks this

stereotype genealogical pattern in half. Accordingly, Genesis 5:32, which precedes the account of the deluge, contains the first two elements observed in the genealogical pattern, noting that (1) Noah was 500 years old, and (2) after that time "he became the father of Shem, Ham, and Japheth." The story of the Flood then follows these details. Finally, Genesis mentions the remaining two elements of Noah's genealogical pattern: (3) "After the flood Noah lived 350 years" and (4) "Altogether, Noah lived 950 years, and then he died" (chap. 9: 28, 29). In this way the writer placed Noah's unforgettable experience in the center of his own genealogy and anchored it to his lifetime. Moreover, as the last verses of chapter 9 complete the information concerning Noah given at the end of chapter 5, they inseparably link the pre-Flood patriarchs with the post-Flood ancestors of God's people.

Chapters 6-9 proceed in a series of paragraphs that we may divide into two groups by the central statement "But God remembered Noah and all the wild animals and the livestock that were with him in the ark" (chap. 8:1). It is the crescendo to which the first group of texts move as the waters swell in destruction and the ark remains the sole source of light and life in the deepening darkness and atmosphere of death. The first group of texts begins with God's decision to unleash the Flood, followed by His announcement to Noah of the event, and concludes by the divine command to enter the boat.

After the assurance that "God remembered Noah," the second group of texts retraces the major events mentioned in the first group in reverse order and falls away in a decrescendo as the waters disappear and the rainbow unveils the new creation. Thus the second group of texts ends with God's telling Noah and his family to leave the vessel and informing them of His decision not to bring another deluge on the world.

The Flood account is a dramatic unity in which the literary movement employs repetition, resumption, recapitulation, and summary. The narrative consists of a sequence of units in which each individual unit has an essential function and thus is indispensable.[18]

The stories of Creation and the Flood complement each other in that both feature supernatural interventions. The former manifests God's supernatural activity in calling human history into existence, while the latter demonstrates the same power in bringing human history to a cataclysmic conclusion. Both acts underscore the fact that God knows no limitations, and they guarantee the success of His promised interventions in the future. Moreover, the events of Genesis 1-9 recording the history of the antediluvians and God's dealings with them contain momentous lessons for us today. In an extended sense Paul's words still apply: "These things happened to them as examples and were written down as warnings for us, on whom the fulfillment of the ages has come. So, if you think you are standing firm, be careful that you don't fall!" (1 Cor. 10:11, 12).

While Genesis depicts the Deluge like a reversal of Creation, the Flood also begins a new creation. Several distinctive phrases and ideas in Genesis 6-9 recall similar words and notions in the Creation story. At the beginning of Creation, waters encompassed the entire globe (Gen. 1:2). God first divided the waters above the expanse from those below the expanse. Next He separated the waters below the expanse so that the dry land might appear (verses 6-10). In the Deluge, however, the waters above reunited with those below once more and covered the planet. God reversed the process of separation that He had effected at Creation. The Bible records that on the day when the floodwaters came on the earth "all the springs of the great deep burst forth, and the floodgates of the heavens were opened. . . . The waters rose and increased greatly on the earth. . . . The waters rose and covered the mountains to a depth of more than twenty feet. . . . The waters flooded the earth. . . . (chap. 7:11, 18, 20, 24).

In the beginning "God created man in his own image, in the image of God he created him; male and female he created them" (chap. 1:27). Assessing the works of His hands and lips, the Creator explained that " 'it was very good' " (verse 31). Yet the prologue to the Flood account notes "how great man's wickedness on the earth had become, and that every inclination of the thoughts of his heart was only evil all the time" (chap. 6:5). "The earth was corrupt in God's sight and was full of violence" (verse 11). The great wickedness was perpetual and had affected almost the whole of society. At the time of the Flood sin had well-nigh obliterated the image of God.

The Hebrew word translated "corrupt" (shachath) in verses 11 and 12 also has the meaning "to destroy" and is rendered thus in the phrase " 'I am surely going to destroy both them and the earth' " (verse 13). Here is a correspondence between human sin and divine punishment. As the contemporaries of Noah destroyed themselves (or "corrupted their ways"), so God would destroy them. The Hebrew word shachath also appears in Psalm 53 (paralleled in Psalm 14), which, though written to address a different historical situation, is an apt commentary on society in the days of the Flood:

"The fool says in his heart, 'There is no God.'
They are corrupt, and their ways are vile;
there is no one who does good.

> God looks down from heaven on the sons of men
> to see if there are any who understand,
> any who seek God.
> Everyone has turned away,
> they have together become corrupt;
> there is no one who does good,
> not even one" (verses 1-3).

Jesus made the following comment on the apathy of the diluvian generation: " 'In the days before the flood, people were eating and drinking, marrying and giving in marriage, up to the day Noah entered the ark; and they knew nothing about what would happen until the flood came and took them all away' " (Matt. 24:38, 39). They were culpable precisely because they had rejected Noah's warning and God's pleas for change. They "disobeyed long ago when God waited patiently in the days of Noah while the ark was being built" (1 Peter 3:20; compare Gen. 6:3).

During the time the descendants of Seth and of Cain formed marriage alliances, the Nephilim were abroad on the earth (see chap. 6:1-4). "Giants" is probably an incorrect translation for the Hebrew word *nephilim*. The word seems to be derived from the verb *naphal* ("to fall"), which might suggest that the *nephilim* were a group of "fallen," "oppressive," or "violent" people. Numbers 13:33 employs the word to designate a group of people related to the "descendants of Anak" who lived among the Canaanites. The Hebrew spies described the Canaanites rather than the Nephilim as frightfully tall and strong (Num. 13:31, 32). Height would have meant little among the races before the Flood, when all were tall in stature. Hence, character rather than stature seems to be in view in this passage. The Nephilim were therefore distinguished by their fallen state and violence. The decline of man originally created in the image of God was so marked at that time that David J. A. Clines suggests that the prologue to the Flood describes a "satanic parody of the doctrine of the image of God in man."

In contrast to that which we read about the heart of Noah's contemporaries, Genesis also records what took place in the heart of God. Whereas man's wickedness on earth had become so great that "every inclination of the thoughts of his heart was only evil all the time[,] the Lord was grieved that he had made man on the earth, and his heart was filled with pain" (Gen. 6:5, 6). Genesis here recites God's affection, grief, and bitter disappointment with humanity.

God found only Noah and his family to be righteous in their generation. "Noah was a righteous man, blameless among the people of his time, and he walked with God" (verse 9). Though Noah was not without faults (see chap. 9:20-24), faith and integrity characterized his life. The hero of the Flood had no claim upon God's favor because of some intrinsic merit of his own. Because he believed and trusted in God Noah was considered righteous and found favor in the eyes of God (chap. 6:8). Similarly, after the Flood the Lord demonstrated His grace and good will *even though* the inclination of man's heart was evil (chap. 8:21). It was *not* Noah's sacrifice that obligated God to restore His relationship with Noah. Rather, the sacrifice offered by Noah provided the occasion at which God in His grace entered into the new relationship with the survivors.

Scripture stresses that Noah was "blameless among the people of his time." In the Bible, "blamelessness" means wholeheartedness rather than absence of sin. Noah had wholeheartedly committed himself to the Lord. Like Enoch, he walked with God, and God was safe in saving him (chap. 6:9; compare chap. 5:22, 24).

The writer to the Hebrews adds the comment "By faith Noah, when warned about things not yet seen, in holy fear built an ark to save his family. By his faith he condemned the world and became heir of the righteousness that comes by faith" (Heb. 11:7). His lifestyle, preaching, and building activity testified to the reality of his faith and therefore distinguished him from his generation.

Genesis 6 teaches the idea of individual responsibility. The fact that only Noah and his family survived the tempest *individually* because they were righteous implies that the rest of his contemporaries were also judged individually. Though the divine judgment may have the appearance of a collective retribution, it was essentially an individual affair. The notion implied in these chapters—that the state of society is a reflection of individual sins and that God holds everyone responsible for his sin—is rather novel in the ancient East.

Noah's salvation was no arbitrary act. God was not capricious in His retribution upon that generation. In this respect the Biblical Flood story differs from the Mesopotamian Flood accounts, which we will discuss in the following chapter. In Genesis the Lord carefully investigated and assessed the attitudes, the behavior, and the motives of the antediluvians. Note the words "The Lord *saw* how great man's wickedness on earth had become." "God *saw* how corrupt the earth had become" (Gen 6:5, 12). The Lord pleaded with Noah's generation to turn from their evil ways and granted them 120 years of probationary time (verse 3; compare 1 Peter 3:19, 20). However, once He had exhausted all avenues, God grievingly announced the impending retribution.

The moral indictment recorded in Genesis 6:1-12

outlines the reason for the Deluge. Such a moral motivation is absent from the Mesopotamian versions of the Flood. The justice of God is stressed in the words spoken to Noah: " 'I am going to put an end to all people, for the earth is filled with violence because of them' " (Gen. 6:13). The Jewish scholar Nahum Sarna observes, "The story of the Flood, like that of Sodom and Gomorrah, presupposes the existence of a universal moral law governing the world for the infraction of which God, the Supreme Judge, brings men to account. It asserts, through the medium of the narrative, that man cannot undermine the moral basis of society without endangering the very existence of civilization. In fact, society, by its own corruption, actually may be said to initiate a process of inevitable retribution." [19]

While the Flood narrative illustrates that evil deserves judgment, it also teaches that divine judgment, though inevitable, is never indiscriminate. Noah and his family escaped the retribution upon an unrepenting world. The hero of the Biblical deluge and his family became the first remnant in Scripture, explicitly stated in the words "Only Noah was left, and those with him in the ark" (chap. 7:23). Later Scripture repeatedly associates the root underlying the verb translated "left" with the concept of the remnant. This earliest occurrence of the remnant theme in the Bible defines a "remnant" as an individual or a group of people who have survived a catastrophe and become the chain that links human existence in the past with human existence in the present and future.

Genesis features Noah and his family in a context of judgment and *salvation.* While Genesis 6-9 deals with the guilt and consequent punishment upon Noah's contemporaries, it stresses the gracious *salvation* of the faithful family. The remnant theme, therefore, has an unmistakable future perspective. The story of Noah opens up the possibility of future existence and survival. Ultimately God's will is seen to be salvation and not doom, giving the remnant theme, beginning with Noah, a pronounced future orientation. The Biblical hero and his family survived, as we have already noted, not because of some inherent merit of their own, but because they stood in a relationship of trust characterized as "righteous" and manifested in a certain lifestyle.

When from a human perspective all seemed to be lost, God's grace, mercy, and faithfulness made possible a new beginning. After Noah had been confined in the ark by the gray curtains of rain, the Lord finally rewarded his patience. "God *remembered* Noah and all the wild animals and the livestock that were with him in the ark" (chap. 8:1). The Lord demonstrated in action His faithfulness to His creatures. He remembered Noah and fulfilled the purpose that He had promised. The springs of the deep and the floodgates of the heavens closed. The rain stopped falling, and the waters began to recede. The entire incident assures us that God will never forget to fulfill His promises.

In the days of Noah "the ark was God's appointed place of salvation, and outside of it there was no safety. And as it was in the days of Noah, so will it be when this present age is brought to an abrupt close at the coming of the Son of man. . . . Those who wish to be saved must avail themselves of the provision God has made for their salvation." [20]

Like Adam, Noah stepped out into a new world once the waters had receded, and he began a new genealogical line. The command first given at Creation, " 'be fruitful and increase in number,' " God once more repeated after the Flood, and it was fulfilled in the genealogical lines and territorial expansions that we shall discuss in greater detail in the following chapter.

A New Beginning

Scholars have discovered reports of destructive floods covering the earth all over the world. However, none parallel the Biblical Flood story as closely as those found in Mesopotamia. Most significant among the latter is the account recorded on the eleventh tablet of the Babylonian *Gilgamesh Epic*. According to this epic the hero of the Babylonian deluge, who was called Utnapishtim, received a warning of the impending destruction and instructions to build a vessel for himself, his family, and for foodstuff. After he had completed the boat and all had boarded the vessel, the tempest began and soon inundated the land, destroying all life upon it.

When the storm had subsided and the ship landed on one of the mountain peaks east of Mesopotamia, Utnapishtim released a dove, then a swallow, and finally a raven. The dove and swallow, which he had sent out at intervals, returned to the vessel. When subsequently he released the raven and it failed to come back, Utnapishtim considered it as an indication that it was safe for all on board to disembark. Upon leaving the ship, the Babylonian hero expressed his gratitude for survival by offering sacrifices to the gods, around which the deities gathered like flies.

Because the currently known forms of the Mesopotamian Flood stories were written before Moses composed the book of Genesis, and since we can recognize several parallels between the Biblical and non-Biblical versions, scholars have suggested that the Old Testament was indebted to the Sumerians and Babylonians for its Flood account. However, a number of major differences exist between the Biblical and non-Biblical stories. First, the Babylonian Flood story is in a context of polytheism in which the different gods behave in a deceptive, cruel, and churlish manner. Second, the deluge occurs because the Mesopotamian gods are capricious and intent on destroying mankind. Indeed, the absence of any moral motivaton for the flood in the Babylonian story distinguishes it clearly from the Biblical account. In the latter the moral reason for the inundation is decisive. Third, the Babylonian tale is essentially a personal story and lacks the *cosmic* dimensions underlying the Biblical account.

Nevertheless, several parallels remain, suggesting that both Biblical and non-Biblical versions have a common source. The worldwide distribution of Flood accounts appears to support this theory. While some of these deluge stories undoubtedly reflect local disasters, the universal occurrence of such narratives tends to support the historicity of Genesis 6-9. The late Gerhard von Rad noted: "It may be said . . . that even natural scientists have not considered the prevailing explanation—that the numerous Flood stories in the world arose from local catastrophes—to be sufficient. . . . On the one hand the distribution of the saga (among Indians, Persians, Africans, Melanesians, and Australians, among the Eskimos, the Kamchatkans, Indians of the Americas, et cetera), on the other hand its remarkable uniformity (flood caused by rain), require the assumption of an actual cosmic experience and a primitive recollection."[21]

On the above assumption of a common source for both the Biblical and non-Biblical Flood stories, the descendants of Noah carried the unforgettable account with them as they spread around the globe, with those residing nearest to the place of disembarkation retaining the most vivid memory of the deluge. Given the testimony of Scripture itself that the majority of Noah's descendants slipped into idolatry and polytheism, the true account of the Flood would have become distorted among them, and the moral motivation for the Flood either lost or deliberately deformed.

Archaeological evidence of thick flood sediments at several ancient Mesopotamian sites (e.g., Ur, Erech, Kish, et cetera) gives no support to the Genesis flood. Such flood levels point merely to local inundations, probably caused by the rising waters of the Euphrates. They in no way substantiate the universal extent of the deluge taught by Scripture.

After the resolution of the Flood, during which the former *Creation* had been *uncreated*, a gracious act of God once more *re-created* the world. The remaining chapters of the primeval history now report conditions upon the earth after the occupants of the ark alighted from their vessel. The experience of the Deluge could have easily generated despair, gloom, and uncertainty in the minds of Noah and his family. Doubt about the future could have consumed their souls had it not been for God's assurance. The rainbow, established by His initiative and as a token of grace that no human effort could procure, was more than a splash of color—it was a reminder of God's goodness. The bow in the clouds gave them hope and assured the postdiluvians of the constant rhythm of seedtime and harvest. Looking upon the rainbow reminded Noah that God is an all-sufficient ground for hope. It guaranteed that God's ordinances would endure and His purposes would come to conclusion.

While the Flood had eliminated sinful men, it had not been able to eradicate sinful nature, as we see vividly illustrated in the story of Noah's drunkenness (Gen. 9:20-27). Scripture faithfully records both the virtues and the vices of its heroes. While the writer of Genesis stresses the integrity of Noah in a corrupt age, it also recognizes his vulnerability. Obviously, neither divine revelation nor spiritual knowledge is ever a guarantee against sin once one provides the enemy of souls with opportunity.

Though the incident of Noah's drunkenness is somewhat peripheral in the context of his total biography, it does teach several significant lessons. First, the experience reveals the tragic loss of dignity suffered by the intoxicated. Noah, who had occupied a place of great respect, lost not only honor but also his sense of decency. Second, the account portrays two attitudes that people display to the sinner. On the one hand we read about Ham, who "saw his father's nakedness and told his two brothers outside" (verse 22). On the other hand the record notes: "But Shem and Japheth took a garment and laid it across their shoulders; then they walked in backward and covered their father's nakedness. Their faces were turned the other way so that they would not see their father's nakedness" (chap. 9:23). Instead of recognizing that because of his failure Noah stood in special need of help, Ham took advantage of his father's plight and exposed his misfortune.

The incident opens to our view the self-righteous, snickering, and gossiping of those spiritual descendants of Ham who exploit the vulnerability of those who have fallen—particularly if such ones have been held in high esteem—and expose them in their nakedness. Yet we also admire the nobility of those who view the sins and failures of their fellow human beings in the context of their lives of integrity. Such accept the admonition of Peter: "Above all, love each other deeply, because love covers over a multitude of sins" (1 Peter 4:8). While we cannot excuse sin, we should aim to examine ourselves humbly, identify sympathetically with the sinner, exhort feelingly, and seek redemptively to cover his or her nakedness.

The table of nations given in Genesis 10 begins with the words "This is the account of Shem, Ham and Japheth, Noah's sons, who themselves had sons after the flood" (verse 1). This verse continues the comment: "The sons of Noah who came out of the ark were Shem, Ham and Japheth. . . . These were the three sons of Noah, and from them came the people who were scattered over the earth" (chap. 9:18, 19).

Both the table of nations in Genesis 10 and the genealogy in Genesis 11 demonstrate the fulfillment of the divine promise and mandate, " 'Be fruitful and increase in number and fill the earth' " (chap. 9:1). The map of nations reveals the geographical expansion of mankind, while the genealogy explains the successions in time. The table of nations becomes the medium through which the writer of Genesis expresses the common descent and fundamental unity of the human race, a theme that he first announced by stating that all men and women descended from Adam and Eve. In reiterating that all peoples came from Noah and his three sons, the narrator once more highlights the interrelatedness of all nations regardless of racial, geographical, or national differences. Centuries later Paul returned to this truth when he proclaimed to the

Athenians, " 'From one man he [i.e., God] made every nation of men, that they should inhabit the whole earth; and he determined the times set for them and the exact places where they should live' " (Acts 17:26).

Genesis 10 and 11 follow each other in order of historical importance rather than chronology, a fact evident from several verses in Genesis 10 that anticipate the division of language reported in chapter 11. Thus we read that from the descendants of Javan "the maritime peoples spread out into their territories by their clans within their nations, *each with its own language*" (verse 5).

Again, "these are the descendants of Ham by their clans and *languages*, in their territories and nations" (verse 20), and "these are the sons of Shem by their clans and *languages*, in their territories and nations" (verse 31). Such hints in regard to the variety of languages suggest that the Tower of Babel episode did not follow the events recorded in chapter 10 in time. Some have suggested that the division of language and the scattering of peoples recorded in Genesis 11:1-9 occurred at the time of Peleg, a thought suggested by the note "Two sons were born to Eber: One was named Peleg, because *in his time* the earth was *divided*" (chap. 10:25).

Genesis 11 introduces the reader to a situation in which "the whole world had one language and a common speech" (verse 1). We may render the Hebrew literally, "the whole world had one lip and one [sort of] words." It suggests the existence of not only one language but even the absence of dialectical differences. Research in comparative grammar tends to support the idea that all known languages are related and descended from a common original.[22]

The descendants of Noah who most probably

migrated to the fertile and open plain of southern Mesopotamia abused the gift of one common and universal language. Once they settled, they resisted God's mandate to " 'fill the earth' " (chap. 9:1). Their resolve, " 'Come, let us build ourselves a city, with a tower that reaches to the heavens, so that we may make a name for ourselves and not be scattered over the face of the whole earth' " (chap. 11:4), directly conflicted with God's purpose that they spread abroad.

The report about the Tower of Babel is a statement about human words and actions (verses 3, 4) balanced with a comment about the words and actions of God (verses 6, 7). "The phrase "Come, let us . . ." (verses 3, 4, 7) and the verb "to scatter" (verses 4, 8, 9) mark both statements. God's actions respond to and correlate with those of the inhabitants of Shinar. Here we see still another clear correspondence between sin and judgment. While mankind arrogantly chose not to be "scattered" in an act of self-serving autonomy, the Lord accomplished the purpose for the world He had envisaged since Creation and reaffirmed after the Flood by scattering them abroad (verse 8). Thus, while Genesis 10 demonstrates the common descent of all peoples, Genesis 11 explains the diversity of peoples and languages that we see today.

Primeval history ends with the genealogy of Shem. The table of nations prepares the reader of Genesis for this sudden turn by arranging the chapter in such a way that the introductory statement, "This is the account of Shem, Ham, and Japheth" (chap. 10:1), expands in *inverted* fashion and discusses Japheth (verses 2-5) and Ham (verses 6-20) before Shem (verses 21-31).

In this way the writer of Genesis narrowed the worldwide sweep of nations and focused on Shem and the immediate ancestors of Abraham, whose story will occupy us presently.

The genealogies recorded in Genesis 5:1-32 and 11:10-26 bind together the stories of Creation, Flood, and patriarchal history. We have already noted that the genealogies are significant because they demonstrate the unity of the human race and the fulfillment of the divine mandate and promise to "be fruitful and increase in number and fill the earth" (chaps. 1:28; 9:1).

In most of the genealogical records in Scripture the inspired writers selected certain names and omitted others. Such omissions become apparent when we examine other scriptural records covering the same period of time. For example, a comparison of Luke's listing of our Lord's earliest ancestors with the genealogy recorded in the Hebrew version of Genesis 11 reveals that Luke added the name Cainan between Arphaxad and Shelah, while the Hebrew writer of Genesis 11 omitted it (compare Gen. 11:12 with Luke 3:35, 36). Similarly, when we put Matthew 1:8—which is part of Jesus' genealogy—alongside 1 Chronicles 3:11, 12 it is evident that Matthew omitted the kings Ahaziah, Joash, and Amaziah between his listing of kings Joram and Uzziah (also known as Azariah). Matthew passed from Joram to Joram's great-great-grandson Uzziah. These and other examples suggest the Bible writers did not intend the genealogies to be full and complete chronological records. The retention of words like *father, son,* and *begat* in the genealogical accounts, despite omissions of names, suggest that the ancient writers employed such terms in the sense of "ancestor" or "descendant" rather than as defining direct lineal predecessors or successors.

The genealogies recorded in Genesis 5 and 11 appear to be arranged schematically. The reference to a set of ten pre-Flood and a set of ten post-Flood patriarchs indicates this. Another example of schematic arrangement in genealogies is the triple pattern of fourteen generations referred to in Matthew 1:17, a structure that we can preserve only if we omit the above-mentioned kings from the record. It is significant that the author of Genesis 5 and 11 nowhere adds the numerical figures together to establish a chronological pattern. This orderly and systematic treatment within the genealogies, however, we should not take as a license to allegorize these records. Whatever interpretation the genealogical patterns or the long ages mentioned in these chapters may suggest to us, Genesis 5 and 11, in the total context of Scripture, must have the last word. The Bible generally, and the genealogies in Genesis specifically, take the individuals mentioned and their life spans literally and seriously.

While the lists of names may appear tedious to the ordinary reader, they reveal that God is personally interested in and concerned for every individual. He values every one of us. He knows us by name and remembers us. Furthermore, the genealogies speak of both death and hope. The repetition "then he died" (Gen. 5:5, 8, 11, et cetera) reminds us of present realities before one day " 'death . . . [is] swallowed up in victory' " (1 Cor. 15:54). However, the genealogies also offer God's guarantee that death is not the bottom line. The refrain "then he died" halts at the startling comment "Enoch walked with God; then he was no more, because God took him away" (Gen. 5:24).

Where others lived on (e.g., see verses 7, 10, 13, et cetera), the Bible states that "Enoch walked with God" (verse 22). "For three hundred years Enoch had been seeking purity of soul, that he might be in harmony with Heaven. For three centuries he had walked with

God. Day by day he had longed for a closer union; nearer and nearer had grown the communion, until God took him to Himself. He had stood at the threshold of the eternal world, only a step between him and the land of the blest; and now the portals opened, the walk with God, so long pursued on earth, continued, and he passed through the gates of the Holy City—the first from among men to enter there." [23]

Though death might presently still reign, God has robbed this enemy of supremacy. Enoch's translation guarantees that one day soon "there will be no more death or mourning or crying or pain, for the old order of things has passed away" (Rev. 21:4).

Faith and Fear

Beginning with the genealogy of Abram, the book of Genesis narrows its perspective from a global vision to the family of faith. With Genesis 12 we close the book of primeval history and open the first page of the volume of patriarchal history. Where previously our eyes rested on God's providence for all nations, Genesis now invites us to concentrate on God's election of the family of promise.

The chosen family appears on the stage of history in response to an act of grace, a fact stressed by the brief but significant note "Now Sarai was barren; she had no children" (Gen. 11:30). The startling comment appears to be in direct conflict with the divine mandate and blessing given at Creation and reiterated after the Flood to " 'be fruitful and increase' " (chaps. 1:28; 9:1). It seems incongruous that the ancestress of the elect people should be barren when she was to become the mother of a nation. Yet it is precisely Sarai's barrenness and Abram's age that highlight the truth that the history of Israel required a divine miracle from its very inception. The same God who brought the world into existence had to speak the creative word to begin Israel. As in Eden and in the days of Noah, history commenced once again entirely by God's grace.

The Lord's choice and call of Abram was equally an

evidence of mercy and grace. The initiative rested entirely with God. He chose Abram and commanded the patriarch to leave home and family (see chap. 12:1). Notice the repeated first person pronoun "I will" in the divine summons to Abram: " 'Go to the land *I will* show you. *I will* make you into a great nation and *I will* bless you; *I will* make your name great. . . . *I will* bless those who bless you, and whoever curses you *I will* curse' " (verses 1-3). The future held out to Abram did not rest on his achievements, merits, or accomplishments, but was solely a gift from God.

The divine speech repeats the words *bless*, *blessing*, or *blessed* five times and announces God's intention for Abram and Sarai. The blessing includes the promise of land and descendants. The Lord pledged that He would lead the patriarch to a land intended for him and that He would make him " 'into a great nation' " (verses 1, 2; compare verse 2 and 4 with chap. 11:30). This story defies the modern notion that the world is closed, fixed, or self-contained. God planned to create miraculously a new community that would live in a country He provided and would rely in faith on His faithfulness.

The Lord further promised Abram, " 'I will make your name great, and you will be a blessing' " (verse 2). The builders in the plain of Shinar decided, " 'Come, let us build ourselves a city, with a tower that reaches to the heavens, so that we may *make a name for ourselves*' " (chap. 11:4). Their self-sufficient effort failed, yet God promised Abram the very renown and preeminence that the builders sought for themselves. History testifies to the fulfillment of God's promise for Abram's name. Millions of Jews, Moslems, and Christians still cherish it.

The intimacy that God envisaged with Abram is

expressed in the statement " 'I will bless those who bless you, and whoever curses you I will curse' " (chap. 12:3). God invited him into such a close friendship that He would consider any blessings granted to Abram as blessings bestowed upon Himself and any insults heaped upon the patriarch as insults thrust upon Himself. Here the Lord announced the theme of salvation and judgment that would unfold in the subsequent history of salvation. Gerhard von Rad suggests that "the promise given to Abraham has significance, however, far beyond Abraham and his seed. God now brings salvation [blessings] and judgment [curses] into history, and man's judgment and salvation will be determined by the attitude he adopts toward this work which God intends to do in history." [24]

The divine speech concludes with a promise: " 'And all peoples on earth *will be blessed* through you' " (verse 3). The Hebrew phrase underlying this translation we may render in the passive as found in the translation just given, or we can reproduce it with the reflexive meaning "By you all the families of the earth *shall bless themselves*." The former rendering is in keeping with the global context of the previous chapters, according to which the nations had been scattered across the face of the whole earth. The Greek translation of this verse follows this meaning, as does also the New Testament (e.g., Acts 3:25). Similarly, Paul notes, "The Scripture foresaw that God would justify the Gentiles by faith, and announced the gospel in advance to Abraham: 'All nations will be blessed through you.' So those who have faith are blessed along with Abraham, the man of faith." Then the apostle decides: "If you belong to Christ, then you are Abraham's seed, and heirs according to the promise" (Gal. 3:8, 9, 29). The promise to Abraham, therefore, turns into a commission according to which the patriarch and his descendants are to live in order to be a blessing to others.

As evident from Stephen's speech delivered centuries later before the Jewish council, Abram's call apparently took place in two stages. Stephen stated, " 'The God of glory appeared to our father Abraham while he was still in Mesopotamia, before he lived in Haran. "Leave your country and your people," God said, "and go to the land I will show you" ' " (Acts 7:2, 3). Stephen's words supplement the Genesis account of Abram's call and suggest that before the summons to leave Haran for Canaan recorded in Genesis 12:1-3 the Lord had already asked him to set out from Ur. Genesis records, "Terah took his son Abram, his grandson Lot son of Haran, and his daughter-in-law Sarai, the wife of his son Abram, and together they set out from Ur of the Chaldeans to go to Canaan. But when they came to Haran they settled there. Terah lived 205 years and, he died in Haran" (chap. 11:31, 32). According to Joshua, Terah, Abram's father, " 'worshiped other gods' " (Joshua 24:2). The practice continued among Abram's relatives who settled in the region of Haran.

Possibly Moses said that Terah took Abram to Haran, rather than the other way around, out of deference to Oriental propriety. The bald statement that a son would take his father may have been offensive. It is clear that after Terah's death God called Abram in Haran to leave his relatives and home for a land that the Lord would show him.

God's instruction to the patriarch was significant. Literally Genesis 12:1 reads, "Go *out of* your land and *from* your relations." The prepositions "out of" and "from" suggest that Abram was to turn his back on the friendly and familiar and step out into the unknown and unwelcome. The Lord instructed him to leave Mesopotamia, where rivers and canals watered the fertile plains and go to a mountainous land, heavily wooded, less fertile, and offering little permanent grazing land. The sophisticated and established society and religion of Mesopotamia simply could not tolerate the challenge of the new religion that God envisaged. At the age of 75 Abram left Haran, having to adjust to a new country, climate, and different customs.

While ambition or an inner restlessness or a yearning to discover new territories motivates some to forsake homeland and relatives, the desire to obey God's will impelled Abram. He did not merely *intend* to go to the land that God would show him, nor did he only *endeavor* to separate his ties from home and family. The patriarch sensed God's voice and left neither questioning nor driven by some momentary enthusiasm. He set out in spite of uncertainty about the speedy fulfillment of the divine promises. "Many are still tested as was Abraham. They do not hear the voice of God speaking directly from the heavens, but He calls them by the teachings of His word and the events of His providence. They may be required to abandon a career that promises wealth and honor, to leave congenial and profitable associations, and separate from kindred, to enter upon what appears to be only a path of self-denial, hardship, and sacrifice. . . . Who is ready at the call of Providence to renounce cherished plans and familiar associations? Who will accept new duties and enter untried fields, doing God's work with firm and willing heart, for Christ's sake counting his losses gain?"[25]

Abram's commitment to the Lord stands in sharp contrast to John Bunyan's character Mr. By-ends, who confesses, " 'Tis true we somewhat differ in religion from those of the stricter sort, yet but in two small points: First, we never strive against wind and tide. Secondly, we are always most zealous when Religion goes in his silver slippers; we love much to walk with him in the street if the sun shines, and the people applaud him." [26]

The patriarch and his wife embraced God's call and promise and responded in faith. Their departure from both Ur and Haran revealed their living relationship with God and demonstrated faith in action. Abram's commitment to the Lord was such that he was willing to forsake the present for the promise of the future.

Unfortunately, the patriachial story does not record any specific names or events that would enable us to correlate it with non-Biblical history. Similarly, we can only estimate the route Abram, Sarai, Lot, and their rather sizable caravan took from Ur to Haran and on into Canaan. All too soon a famine in Canaan drove Abram's camp to Egypt (Gen. 12:10).

Once he arrived in Egypt, this giant of belief struggled with faith and faithfulness. Intent on securing his own survival in the face of hunger, he momentarily lost sight of God's promise and relied on his own wisdom and resources. Sarai's beauty—given the extended life span of the patriarchs, her 60s possibly corresponded with our 30s or 40s—did not go unnoticed (verses 11-14). Fearing for his life, Abram sought to pass Sarai, who actually was his half sister, off as his full sister instead of his wife. Faith in the Lord succumbed to fright as the patriarch used one half of the truth to conceal the other half that she was also his wife. Once entangled in the net of sin, he was unable to refuse the customary dowry given the patriarch by Pharaoh for his *own* wife (verse 16). What shame and dishonor Abram had cast upon his God as the man of the world exposed the man of God as a cheat. Indeed, Abram's deviousness could have ended in disaster and destroyed God's very purpose for the chosen people. His lapse could have cost him the loss of both his wife and the expected and hoped-for son.

Genesis 12 illustrates realistically and vividly how suddenly a spiritual giant whose commitment one can only admire may fail. Moreover, it is incredible, yet true, that both the father and son should go over the same ground and fall again (see verse 2; Chap. 26:7). Abram had to learn that human schemes, even in times of desperation, are only a poor substitute for faith.

However, the account is not primarily about him, but about God. The focus is not so much upon the patriarch's faith and lapse of courage and honesty as upon God's faithfulness. Though Abram failed Him, the Lord would not fail Abram, even if it took plagues to restore Sarai and a deportation to get both back to the chosen land (see chap. 12:17, 20). The heavenly Father would keep His promises even if the patriarch did not believe them.

In contrast to the example of calculating self-serving stands Abram's magnanimity when faced by the choice of land for his and Lot's flocks and herds (chap. 13). Whereas the patriarch's inability to trust described in Genesis 12 caused him to fear, here his confident trust in the same promises made him generous. While in Genesis 12 Abram relied on his own shrewdness and was prepared to sacrifice others for his own well-being, in Genesis 13 he took no thought for himself, and the patriarch's unselfishness became a virtue worthy of emulation.

In an interesting analysis of these two chapters Walter Brueggemann suggested that the writer "comes to the point" of Genesis 13 in verses 14-17.[27] They record the Lord's speech to Abram after Lot had made his choice and departed. God challenged Abram to raise his eyes and behold the land that He would give to the patriarch and to his offspring. The promises of land and descendants were completely unexpected, for Abram had no idea about the outcome of the risk he took when he said to Lot, " 'Is not the whole land before you? Let's part company. If you go to the left, I'll go to the right; if you go to the right, I'll go to the left' " (verse 9).

The decision uncle and nephew made was ultimately between "faith" and "sight." Lot saw a well-watered and fertile valley that would fatten his herds, but he failed to consider what it would do to his family. For him the valley before him comprised the Promised Land. His only question was "Will it pay?" not "Is it right?" Soon Lot's clever choice turned into the wrong one, and the presumed advantages into disadvantages.

By contrast, Abram by faith looked beyond the immediate gains and sought only the righteousness of God, and he discovered that God had added the "rest." The patriarch's choice graphically exemplifies the words of Jesus " 'So do not worry, saying, "What shall we eat?" or "What shall we drink?" or "What shall we wear?" For the pagans run after all these things, and your heavenly Father knows that you need them. But seek first his kingdom and his righteousness, and all these things will be given to you as well' " (Matt. 6:31-33).

The superiority of Abram's decision over that of Lot the following chapter (Genesis 14) illustrates. During a campaign of five kings from the east, the raiders took Lot, who by now resided in Sodom, captive and marched him away with his fellow townspeople. The

Bible simply records, "They also carried off Abram's nephew Lot and his possessions, since he was living in Sodom" (verse 12). The enjoyment of his choice of real estate had been short-lived.

Hearing of the incident, Abram and his friends rallied to rescue the prisoners. The patriarch's attitude demonstrates the fact that he took his social responsibilities to his fellowmen as seriously as his obligations to God. The Lord blessed the attempt with success (verses 15, 16).

Upon his return, Abram magnanimously returned the captured goods to those who had been despoiled. It revealed that he had far loftier motives than to enter merely into a plundering expedition so customary in those days. Though the king of Sodom offered Abram the goods that the patriarch had retaken, the latter declined them. The man of God would not accept the idolatrous king's gift, for he did not want to obligate himself to the monarch. He resolved, " 'I will accept nothing belonging to you, not even a thread or the thong of a sandal, so that you will never be able to say, "I made Abram rich" ' " (verse 23). Abram's example cautions us when we are tempted to receive gifts that may have unacceptable strings attached to them, particularly from those who sense no commitment to God.

Sometime after the military expedition against the five eastern kings and the refusal to accept the material reward offered by the Sodomite monarch, fears, discouragement, and doubt overwhelmed the progenitor of Israel. Sarai was still barren, and both of them were growing older.

The apparent delay of the divine promise challenged his faith, and the fear of reprisal for his military involvement bore him down. How could he continue to believe in God's promises when all the evidence seemed to point against their fulfillment?

In a vision the Lord sought to relieve His trusted friend of his anxieties. He said, "'Do not be afraid, Abram. I am your shield, your very great reward'" (chap. 15:1). In his moment of trial God reassured the patriarch that He Himself would be his protection. Moreover, God would far exceed the material rewards that Abram had spurned from the king of Sodom.

However, Abram argued back that rewards would be of little use to him as long as he had no son—as long as only a servant could benefit from his possessions. In reply the Lord assured Abram, "'A son coming from your own body will be your heir'" (verse 4). In order to seal His words, God challenged the man to look at the starlit sky, and then He commented, "'So shall your offspring be'" (verse 5). The Lord, who had created the stars beyond number, could cause another genesis and give an old and barren couple a son. Abram believed, and his unqualified trust in God's word became the basis for the Pauline doctrine of justification by faith (compare Romans 4 and Galatians 3). In the vision the Lord also repeated the promise regarding land and sealed His pledge with a solemn covenant ritual. The ritual assured Abram of ownership, which the later conquest under Joshua would convert into actual possession of the territory.

Nevertheless, God introduced a new element into the promise of land. A delay would occur before Abram's descendants could receive the fulfillment of the promise. It would not be because of the slow growth of Abram's family, but because "'the sin of the Amorites has not yet reached its full measure'" (verse 16). However, God's justice would know neither haste nor delay. The divine judgment would be fair and just to both the righteous and the wicked.

This moral rationalization for the delay in the promise is an evidence that Abram's children did not inherit the land because of any inherent superiority or military prowess on their part, or even because of some divine favoritism. The passage prevented any conceit on the part of the later Israelites. Indeed, God would judge Israel by the same moral standards that He had applied to the Amorites (compare Deut. 9:4-6; Lev. 18:28).

Both seed and land were gifts that could not be forced. Faith had to wait through the delay and rely entirely on God's word. The Lord had promised and given an unqualified commitment (Gen. 15:18-21). Abram must reciprocate in complete trust.

Promise and Peril

Ten years had passed since Abram had separated from his relatives and his homeland. For a decade he had journeyed, constantly expecting the fulfillment of God's promise of a son. Yet Sarai, who had been barren before they left Haran, still remained childless. The Bible records laconically, "Now Sarai, Abram's wife, had borne him no children" (Gen. 16:1).

Sarai sensed that with advancing age she had to take matters into her own hands. She advised her husband, "'The Lord has kept me from having children. Go, sleep with my maidservant; perhaps I can build a family through her'" (verse 2). In a society that regarded childlessness as a disgrace, she took the desperate stand of unbelief. After years of fruitless expectation, she had convinced herself that the Lord kept her from having children. In frustration Sarai resorted to the custom of concubinage, in which a mistress would ask her husband to consort with her female servant. Several texts from the ancient East seem to suggest that several national groups practiced concubinage as a social institution.

The eighteenth century B.C. law code of Hammurabi stipulated that priestesses of a certain rank who were free to marry but not to have children to their husbands could provide their spouses with maidservants for the purpose of bearing children. Should such a slave have children and then become overbearing and claim equality with her mistress, the mistress was free to demote the slave to her former status of servitude.[28]

From the middle of the second millennium B.C. comes a Hurrian legal text discovered at the city of Nuzi that deals even more closely with the situation here. It reads: "[Miss] Kelim-ninu has been given in marriage to [Mr.] Shennima. . . . If Kelim-ninu does not bear [children] Kelim-ninu shall acquire a woman of the land of Lullu [i.e., a slave girl] as wife for Shennima, and Kelim-ninu may not send the offspring away."[29]

According to this law a childless woman was obliged to supply her husband with a concubine in order to raise up children. Though Sarai's situation does not parallel exactly with the cases cited above, the Mesopotamian laws reflect situations of concubinage that suggest her plans in providing her spouse with children were at least compatible with contemporary customs.

The voice of reason took precedence over the divine word. Human manipulation raced ahead of God as both Abram and Sarai resorted to their own schemes and impatiently ignored His promise. Their efforts at self-help provided the basis for Paul's attack on righteousness by works. The apostle argued that "Abraham had two sons, one by the slave woman and the other by the free woman. His son by the slave woman was born in the ordinary way; but his son by the free woman was born as the result of a promise. These things may be taken figuratively, for the women represent two covenants. One covenant is from Mount Sinai and bears children who are to be slaves: This is Hagar. Now Hagar stands for Mount Sinai in Arabia and corresponds to the present city of Jerusalem, because she is in slavery with her children. But the Jerusalem that is above is free, and she is our mother. . . . Now you, brothers, like Isaac, are children of promise" (Gal. 4:22-28).

For the apostle, any effort at self-help in one's relationship with God is incompatible with the way of the Lord. Abram had to learn that the divine promise of seed would be accomplished through a miracle and not through human devising, regardless of how acceptable such efforts might be in the eyes of the world. The patriarch could neither foreshorten the waiting period nor assist God by either accepting his servant Eliezer as his heir or by regarding the son of a slave maid as the promised seed.

His mistake caused much heartache for all concerned. Sarai's idea, bereft of heaven's blessing, resulted in irreversible pain to herself, her husband, her handmaid, and Ishmael. The Bible faithfully records Sarai's harshness to Hagar when the latter became pregnant and overbearing in her attitude toward her mistress. "Sarai mistreated Hagar; so she fled from her" (Gen. 16:6). The reader is left in no doubt as to where the sympathy of Scripture lies. Genesis clearly reveals God's compassion with the weak and suffering. The angel of the Lord found Hagar on the road back to her homeland, manifested himself to the lowly slave, and delivered words of comfort and hope. It is plain from the account that the God of Abram was also the God of Hagar the Egyptian. The same compassionate God showed an equal concern for the yet-unborn Ishmael who would never be a part of the camp of Israel.

A further thirteen years passed after Sarai's ill-fated experiment and the birth of Ishmael before the Lord revealed Himself once more to Abram (chap. 17:1). In contrast to the patriarch's frailty, God identified Himself as the Mighty One and reiterated the covenant that He had made with Abram previously (chapter 15). The covenant combined both *promises* initiated by God under the heading " 'as for me' " (chap. 17:4-8) and *stipulations* laid upon Abraham introduced by the words " 'as for you' " (verses 9-14).

God repeated and expanded the promises of posterity and land. The Lord informed Abram that Sarai, and not another woman, would be the mother of his expected son (verse 16). He added that their posterity would multiply into nations and that they would give rise to royalty (verses 6, 16). To commemorate the extension of the promised "seed," the Lord now changed the names of both Abram and Sarai.

In Scripture and the ancient near East the giving of a name served more than the purpose of identification—it also invested a person with certain characteristics. Conversely, "to cut off a name" amounted to the annihilation of a person (e.g., Deut. 7:24). Hence, the giving or change of a name was very significant. When the "heretic" Pharaoh of Egypt Amenhotep IV (meaning "[the god] Amon is satisfied") changed his allegiance to the god or sun disk Aten, he also altered his name to Akh-en-Aten (meaning "He who is serviceable to the Aten" or "It goes well with the Aten") to signify the beginning of a new era. Daniel and his friends received new names to herald a new sphere of activity in their lives (Dan. 1:7). God changed Jacob's name to Israel to signify the transformaton of his life (Gen. 32:28).

Similarly, the Lord altered Abram's name (perhaps meaning "the father is exalted") to Abraham after God announced that he would be " 'the father of many nations'" (chap. 17:4). Though given our present knowledge of Hebrew the name Abraham does not appear to signify etymologically "father of a multitude," it is clearly the interpretation given by the Bible writer (verse 5). The new name reflects the patriarch's destiny and reminds one of the initial promise, " 'I will make you into a great nation and I will bless you; I will make your name great'" (chap. 12:2). The name Sarah did not involve any marked change. Whereas Sarai ("my princess") probably identified her as specifically Abram's princess, the name Sarah (meaning "a princess") attributed to her dignity in her own right.

While thirteen years previously God guaranteed His covenant to Abraham through a covenant ritual (chapter 15), the Lord now invited the patriarch to demonstrate *his* commitment to God through the rite of circumcision. God ordained the rite—widely practiced by Israel's neighbors—as an everlasting institution and invested it with new meaning. Circumcision as a "'sign of the covenant'" was the pledge of committed faith in which the individual yielded both his affections and will to the covenant partner (chap. 17:11). The practice was therefore an act of dedication to and identification with the covenant community.

Moreover, God declared, "'Any uncircumcised male, who has not been circumcised in the flesh, will be cut off from his people; he has broken my covenant'" (verse 14). While God solely initiated the covenant relationship—an aspect stressed almost exclusively in chapters 12:1-3 and 15:12-18—Abraham and his descendants could benefit by the covenant blessings only *on condition* of accepting its terms. Failure to comply with the institution of circumcision designated a deliberate choice by which the individual renounced the offered relationship and surrendered any hope of being a beneficiary of the promised blessing.

God gave the institution to enrich the faith of Abraham and his posterity. However, a symbol can lose its intent when practiced merely for its own sake. As such the sign becomes empty in meaning and may paralyze rather than enliven. This is precisely what happened to the symbol of circumcision as time passed by. Circumcision had taken on a life of its own and for this reason caused a controversy in the early Christian church (see Acts 15:1-5).

Paul repeatedly reprimanded those who demonstrated a wrong attitude toward circumcision. He wrote, "Circumcision has value if you observe the law, but if you break the law, you have become as though you had not been circumcised. If those who are not circumcised keep the law's requirements, will they not be regarded as though they were circumcised? The one who is not yet circumcised physically and yet obeys the law will condemn you who, even though you have the written code and circumcision, are a lawbreaker. A man is not a Jew if he is only one outwardly, nor is circumcision merely outward and physical. No, a man is a Jew if he is one inwardly; and circumcision is circumcision of the heart, by the Spirit, not by the written code. Such a man's praise is not from men, but from God" (Rom. 2:25-29).

Signs and symbols may still lose their intent today. Thus the ordinance of baptism, rather than designating entry into a new life and loyalty to a new community, may become an empty rite. Similarly, we may forget the significance of the Sabbath and turn it into no more than an instrument of oppression or uniformity. It is our duty to guard against anything that will cause a symbol to lose its meaning, and to do everything we can to preserve the vitality of the God-given sign in both our life and worship.

Both Abraham and Sarah were models of disbelief rather than faith. "Abraham fell facedown; he laughed and said to himself, 'Will a son be born to a man a hundred years old? Will Sarah bear a child at the age of ninety?' And Abraham said to God, 'If only Ishmael might live under your blessing!'" (Gen. 17:17, 18). Our sympathy extends to the patriarch, who was unable to trust. Both he and his wife had become so accustomed to their barrenness that they had resigned themselves to the hopelessness of never having their own child. Abraham simply appealed to Ishmael as an alternative to the divine promise. In response God challenged the patriarch to a radical faith, "'Yes, but your wife Sarah will bear you a son, and you will call him Isaac'" (verse 19). The choice of Isaac over Ishmael did not imply the latter's racial inferiority—rather, it indicated whom God would use in His elective purpose. Later history substantiated the wisdom of His choice.

Sarah found God's challenge to her faith some months later at the entrance of Abraham's tent near the trees of Mamre equally trying. The promise "'I will surely return to you about this time next year, and Sarah your wife will have a son'" was beyond reason and belief (chap. 18:10). Having waited for more than a quarter of a century for the fulfilment of the promise, she discovered faith to be a stumbling block. In her hopelessness she resisted hope and laughed at God's words.

In His mercy and patience God did not reject Sarah in her incredulity. He merely asked, "'Is anything too hard for the Lord?'" (verse 14). His query has become one of the greatest statements of Scripture. It met the old couple's attitude head on and disarmed their protest. The divine statement was *not* an assertion or proclamation but a question—because a question requires a decision. The way Abraham and Sarah would respond to the Lord's inquiry would determine all else. It is still the great and unavoidable question that every one of us must answer. Our response will indicate whether we consider our universe to be closed and hopeless, or open to God's action.

The Lord's question points up the stark contrast between human weakness and impotence and divine strength and omnipotence. In her unbelief Sarah missed those indications that testified to the divine origin of her visitors. Had the guests not revealed knowledge of her name and of her laughter? Had they not read her inner thoughts of incredulity? (verses 9, 12-14). Such things should have been a sign to her that God could perform the greater miracle of bringing life from a seemingly dead womb. The attitude of the matriarch stands in sharp contrast to that of Mary, the mother of our Lord. When the angel Gabriel announced the birth of Jesus, Mary responded: " 'May it be to me as you have said' " (Luke 1:38); compare verse 45). Generations ever since have equally confessed that " 'nothing is impossible with God' " (Luke 1:37; see also Mark 10:27). If God is God, then He cannot be limited by our human expectations.

While the heavenly visitor left Sarah without her answer to His question, Scripture indicates that Abraham no longer shared her doubts. Paul comments that Abraham, without his faith weakening, "faced the fact that his body was as good as dead—since he was about a hundred years old—and that Sarah's womb was also dead. Yet he did not waver through unbelief regarding the promise of God, but was strengthened in his faith and gave glory to God, being fully persuaded that God had power to do what he had promised" (Rom. 4:19-21).

In an insightful commentary on our passage Walter Brueggemann observes that the account does not imply that faith makes every *desirable* thing possible. *Not everything is promised.* "What is 'possible' is characterized only as everything promised by God. That is, only what corresponds to God's good purposes is possible."[30] To the disciples seeking salvation Jesus promised that that which is impossible with men is possible with God (Mark 10:27).

Recognizing our human limitations, God treats us with tenderness, patience, and compassion—as He clearly revealed in His dealings with Abraham and Sarah. Nevertheless, the compassionate God is also the righteous judge concerned about the world's wickedness. The story of Sodom and Gomorrah brings to view this second aspect of God's character. The inhabitants of the cities of the sinful valley lacked what God had found in Abraham. The Lord trusted that Abraham would " 'direct his children and his household after him to keep the way of the Lord by doing what is right and just' " (Gen. 18:19). But the Sodomites "were wicked and were sinning greatly against the Lord" (chap. 13:13).

God told Abraham, " 'The outcry against Sodom and Gomorrah is so great and their sin so grievous' " (chap. 18:20; compare chap. 19:13). The Hebrew word translated "outcry" implies their heinous moral and social corruption and disregard of basic human rights as well as their callous insensitivity to others (compare Ex. 3:7; 22:21-23; Isa. 5:7, et cetera). The unnatural vice of the Sodomites expressed in their intended homosexual gang-rape was simply one manifestation of their depravity. The "outcry" of the Sodomites was equivalent to the "violence" of the antediluvians, and both the story of the Flood and the account of the Sodomites have as their foundation the "existence of a moral law of universal application for the infraction of which God holds all men answerable."[31]

Against this background Abraham speaks of God as the " 'Judge of all the earth' " (Gen. 18:25). Abraham, the father of the elect, who pleaded for an utterly depraved people, rested his whole case on the conviction that God had a passion for righteousness. Both Abraham's family and the people of Canaan were subject to divine righteousness. God's righteousness we see demonstrated by the fact that He personally investigated the outcry that had reached Him (verses 20, 21). Furthermore, it was clear that the wickedness of the Sodomites was all-inclusive (chap. 19:4). Thus the book of Genesis stresses repeatedly that the righteous Judge is not capricious, and though He has all power, He will not use it indiscriminately.

However, righteousness blends with mercy even in the story of Sodom and Gomorrah. The account illustrates that God takes no pleasure in the death of the wicked. He desires that the unrighteous turn from their ways and live, for He *values* the *life* of the righteous *more than* He craves for the *destruction* of the wicked, a truth immortalized in the story of Lot. The man, whom not even warnings of fire and brimstone could persuade to become a pilgrim, was saved purely by God's grace and the intercessory prayers of his uncle (verses 16, 29). Once more God *remembered*, and a remnant was saved (verse 29).

The Pain of Parenthood

Finally Isaac was born. Twenty-five long and weary years had lapsed since God first told Abraham, " 'I will make you into a great nation' " (Gen. 12:2). The heavenly messenger had announced, " 'I will surely return to you about this time next year, and Sarah your wife will have a son' " (chap. 18:10). Now the record states, "Sarah became pregnant and bore a son to Abraham in his old age, *at the very time* God had promised him" (chap. 21:2). The promise had been fulfilled right on time.

Isaac's birth was nothing less than a miracle. The narrator takes pains to highlight the amazement that it caused. The Bible speaks of the "old age" of Abraham and adds that he was "a hundred years old" when Isaac was born to him (verses 2, 5). Sarah exclaimed, " 'Who would have said to Abraham that Sarah would nurse children? Yet I have borne him a son in his old age' " (verse 7). Only now that human ingenuity and man-made schemes had come to an end could the participants fully appreciate the divine intervention. God had broken through the boundaries of natural law and human reason.

Somewhat self-consciously Sarah said, " 'God has brought me laughter, and everyone who hears about this will laugh with me' " (verse 6). The laughable had finally become believeable reality. Isaac's name, meaning "laughter" would remain a constant reminder of his parents' struggle between faith and unbelief. However, pride and joy flooded the mother's heart, and later Bible writers recall this moment as one of the happiest events in Sarah's life. Isaiah reflected on her experience when he wrote, "'Sing, O barren woman, you who never bore a child; burst into song, shout for joy, you who were never in labor; because more are the children of the desolate woman than of her who has a husband'" (Isa. 54:1; compare Gal. 4:27).

As time passed, tensions developed between the two half brothers. Ishmael must have realized that his younger brother would replace him in the right of inheritance. The conflict came to a head at a feast celebrating the weaning of Isaac and resulted in Sarah's request that her husband expel Hagar and Ishmael. As cruel as this ejection sounds to our modern ears, Sarah may well have acted within the context of contemporary ancient Near Eastern law.

The record refuses to conceal the pain that wrenched the heart of the father: "The matter distressed Abraham greatly because it concerned his son" (Gen. 21:11). Ishmael and his mother had to leave, but not without God's assurance to the grieving father that his son to Hagar would share at least partially in the promise made to Abraham. God comforted the distressed man with the statement, "'I will make the son of the maidservant into a nation also, because he is your offspring'" (verse 13). Mercifully, Scripture clothes the departure of Hagar and Ishmael from Abraham in silence. Only imagination can surmise the feelings that raged in the father's troubled breast. He reaped what he had sown and paid a bitter price for an ill-considered course of action.

Two decades after Isaac's birth and some thirteen years after Ishmael's expulsion Abraham endured another test involving his second son. It would be the fiercest trial of his life as God called him to sacrifice his long-awaited son, Isaac, in the region of Moriah (Genesis 22). At the time of the divine command the patriarch had reached the age of 120 years.[32] He no longer enjoyed the vigor of manhood with which to meet hardship, difficulties, danger, and afflictions. "God had reserved His last, most trying test for Abraham until the burden of years was heavy upon him, and he longed for rest from anxiety and toil."[33]

While human sacrifices had not been uncommon among Israel's neighbors, particularly among the Canaanites, it seemed a price too great to demonstrate one's fervor and devotion to God. The command to offer up Isaac must have appeared totally irrational. Had God not promised that through Isaac Abraham's descendants would be named? Now the death of the young man would nullify that promise. The Lord's command simply clashed with His promise. With no descendants, there could be no future. Was the Lord reversing the process and returning the patriarchal family to barrenness? Had the pilgrimage that began with Sarah's barrenness been for naught? Had Abraham not already paid keenly for his moments of unbelief and accepted the results of his actions?

Never had the anvil of the patriarch's faith been struck by a blow so heavy. How could the hands that had caressed, held, and comforted the lad take his life? Isaac was not simply a son—the young man was his only son, whom he loved; he was the boy of miracle and promise!

The old man had heard the voice of God repeatedly, and his mind had no doubt as to who had uttered the command " 'Take your son, your only son Isaac, whom you love, and go to the region of Moriah. Sacrifice him there as a burnt offering on one of the mountains I will tell you about'" (chap. 22:2). That same voice had imparted comfort, hope, grace, and direction in the past to the patriarch. He must advance as commanded, and he dared not trust his feelings or delay. Neither could he afford to talk about it with Sarah, who might only seek to dissuade and hinder him.

The journey from Beersheba across the rugged and stony mountains only added weight to the already heavy paternal heart. The Bible reports the exchange of only a few words as father and son traveled to the region of Moriah. Abraham could not bring himself to reveal the full intent of the mission to his son. The doubt and unbelief whispered to him by Satan heightened the father's anguish. No relief came to his soul as he hoped that a heavenly messenger would call a halt to the march. The joyous songs of the birds along the route must have seemed like cruel mockery. The surrender of the life of the promising and radiant youth—tanned, upright, and full of plans for the future—as a demonstration of his father's devotion to God seemed too costly a price.

Once more the record mercifully veils the last few moments shared by father and son. One can only admire the 20-year-old youth surrendering himself willingly to his aged father. Evidently Abraham had been successful in passing his most precious legacy— his total faith and commitment to God—on to his son. Isaac had willingly accepted that heritage of trust in God. As Abraham raised the knife he demonstrated unequivocally and once and for all that absolutely nothing was more precious to him than God.

The inward intention, the sacrifice made in spirit,

God valued and accepted as the act itself. The angel of the Lord called out to him from heaven, " 'Abraham! Abraham! . . . Do not lay a hand on the boy. . . . Do not do anything to him. Now I know that you fear God, because you have not withheld from me your son, your only son' " (verses 11, 12).

Genesis 22 reveals the true nature of faith. One could give no better example of the relationship of faith and obedience. "By faith Abraham, when God tested him, offered Isaac as a sacrifice. He who had received the promises was about to sacrifice his one and only son, even though God had said to him, 'It is through Isaac that your offspring will be reckoned.' Abraham reasoned that God could raise the dead, and figuratively speaking, he did receive Isaac back from death" (Heb. 11:17-19).

Statements of faith punctuated Abraham's pilgrimage to the Moriah region. On the third day the patriarch instructed his servants, " 'Stay here with the donkey while I and the boy go over there. We will worship and then *we will come back* to you' " (Gen. 22:5). Abraham's mind had no doubt that both father and son would return from the sacrifice. Again, when asked by Isaac, " 'Where is the lamb for the burnt offering?' " he responded, " 'God himself will provide the lamb for the burnt offering, my son' " (verses 7, 8).

Abraham's willingness to act out his faith and obey God's command to sacrifice his own boy demonstrates how serious faith is. Faith is not passive in posture or merely cerebral. It is dynamic and finds its fullest expression in the realm of action. The patriarch demonstrated his faith in his willingness to give to God his most precious gift. He would hold back nothing. In Abraham's experience faith and obedience were inseparable. Paul, whose fascination with Abraham is understandable, considered faith to be so dynamic that he described it as obedience—meaning, of course, surrender to God's word in the good news (e.g., Rom. 1:5). The apostle applauded a "faith expressing itself through love" (Gal. 5:6). James added, "Was not our ancestor Abraham considered righteous for what he did when he offered his son Isaac on the altar? You see that his faith and his actions were working together, and his faith was made complete by what he did" (James 2:21, 22; compare John 8:39). Faith for Abraham, Paul, and James was *not a meritorious* work, but a *re*action to God's initial promise and action. It was a total surrender to both the gift and claims of God.

The divine demand to sacrifice Isaac seriously tested the "father of the faithful." Testing takes place when a single God insists on individual trust and uncompromising fidelity. It is the reason why such trials do not occur in religions of tolerance. They arise when it is appealing to discover easier and less-demanding alternatives to God and His will. Abraham's particular test revealed that his faith was no shallow or one-dimensional piety. Like Job, he was prepared to trust God, who both gives and takes away. But finally the trial of faith ended, and the heavenly voice declared, " 'Now I know that you fear God, because you have not withheld from me your son, your only son' " (Gen. 22:12).

In His grace God Himself *provided* the sacrifice which the grateful father offered "as a b rnt offering *instead* of his son" (verse 13). The literary structure of the episode is significant, as it highlights Abraham's belief that God would provide the lamb for the burnt offering. Brueggemann has divided Genesis 22:1-12 into three series of summonses, responses, and addresses.[34] The first series begins with a summons by God and

Araham's response, followed by the Lord's command (verses 1, 2). The third series commences with the summons of the angel and the old man's response, succeeded by the angel's announcement to free the son (verse 11, 12). The central series opens with Isaac's word to his father and Abraham's reply, followed by the son's question (verse 7). However, in this second series the threefold pattern already noted in the first and third series is extended by a *fourth* element, which states Abraham's conviction: "'God himself will provide the lamb for the burnt offering, my son'" (verse 8). This last statement featured in the very center of the episode falls outside of the normal literary structure of the series and is noteworthy because it highlights unmistakably the patriarch's faith that God would take care of their needs. We may diagram the structure in the following way:

Series 1	*Series 2*	*Series 3*
1. Summons by God (verse 1)	1. Summons by Isaac (verse 7)	1. Summons by angel (verse 11)
2. Response by Abraham (verse 1)	2. Response by Abraham (verse 7)	2. Response by Abraham (verse 11)
3. Address by God (verse 2)	3. Address by Isaac (verse 7)	3. Address by angel (verse 12)
	4. *Statement by Abraham* (verse 8)	

Given the divine provision, Abraham called that place "'The Lord will provide.'" At the time the writer penned his account, he added, "And to this day it is said, 'On the mountain of the Lord it will be provided'" (verse 14).

The eye of faith looks beyond the ram to a Son who

died *instead* of Abraham's *sons and daughters* when once again the Lord provided on Mount Moriah. Abraham's experience on the hill enabled him to taste something of that future ordeal when the heavenly Father provided His only Son to die for mankind (compare John 8:56). No hand then stayed the brutal and unjust ordeal or removed the bitter cup. To save humanity and win the undivided affection of the universe, Jesus yielded up His life. Thus God satisfied justice and displayed love, for "God demonstrates his own love for us in this: While we were still sinners, Christ died for us" (Rom. 5:8). Overwhelmed by such divine concern, Paul wrote, "What, then, shall we say in response to this? *If God is for us, who can be against us?* He who did not spare his own Son, but gave him up for us all—how will he not also, along with him, graciously give us all things?" (chap. 8:31, 32).

Genesis 12 and 22 contain several remarkable parallels and thus form a literary envelope around the spiritual odyssey of the progenitor of God's people. While Genesis 12 presents the call out of Haran and thus the effective start of the pilgrimage, Genesis 22 offers the climactic event in Abraham's life in the call to sacrifice Isaac. Both chapters begin with a summons to go forth. In the former chapter God invited Abraham to go forth " 'to the land I will show you' " (Gen. 12:1). In the latter chapter He asked the patriarch to go forth " 'to the region of Moriah' " to " 'one of the mountains I will tell you about' " (chap. 22:2). In neither instance does God state the precise terminal point of the journey.

The additional details given heighten the drama of the event. As Abraham set out from Haran the Lord instructed him, "Leave your country, your people and your father's household" (chap. 12:1). In the climactic trial of his life God commanded, " 'Take your son, your only son Isaac, whom you love' " (chap. 22:2). At the very beginning of the pilgrimage a son left his father forever. Similarly, at the end of the spiritual journey, father and son once more prepared to part forever.

Abraham's wandering commenced with the erection of an altar to the Lord near "the great tree of Moreh at Shechem" (chap. 12:6, 7) and climaxed with the building of his last recorded altar on the heights of Moriah (see chap. 22:9-14). Both chapters recite strikingly similar blessings (see chaps. 12:2, 3 and 22:17, 18). In fact, Genesis 22 takes up the promise " 'I will make you into a great nation and I will bless you' " (chap. 12:2) and extends it to " 'I will surely bless you and make your descendants as numerous as the stars in the sky and as the sand on the seashore' " (chap. 22:17). Likewise, the Lord repeats and modifies the promise " 'All peoples on earth will be blessed *through you*' " (chap. 12:3) in the words " 'And *through your offspring* all nations on earth will be blessed, because you have obeyed me' " (chap. 22:18).

Abraham's spiritual pilgrimage began and ended with divine communications that challenged him to make agonizing decisions. In both cases the patriarch determined to follow the invitation of the Lord loyally. Within the borders of Genesis 12 and 22 are recorded the essence of the patriarch's struggles and path of faith. One commences, the other closes, with the glorious promises of blessing, posterity, and land.

The Abraham narrative ends with the report of Sarah's death and burial (chapter 23), the selection of the right bride for Isaac (chapter 24), and the record of Abraham's death (chapter 25). The expression of Abraham's grief over his wife's death is poignant. She had shared in the uncertainties of Canaan, suffered the stigma of childlessness, lied for her husband, and experienced years of wistfulness and disappointment. Her great strength had been her fidelity to and love for her spouse. The cave that Abraham bought for Sarah's burial and for a family sepulchre became the first place of real estate he would own in the Promised Land.

In order to secure the succession of the line of promise the aged father had to find the right wife for Isaac. As he commissioned his trusted servant he was totally convinced that God would bless the mission with success. His *last recorded words* are a veritable testimony to his complete trust in God: " 'The Lord, the God of heaven, who brought me out of my father's household and my native land and who spoke to me and promised me on oath, saying, "To your offspring I will give this land"—he will send his angel before you so that you can get a wife for my son from there' " (chap. 24:7). It stands in stark contrast to the first words attributed to Abraham, which reveal his doubts in the promise of God (chap. 15:2, 8). Finally, the doubter had become the man of faith.

Once all that had been accomplished, Abraham could breathe his last. The Bible says he "died at a good old age, an old man and full of years" (chap. 25:8).

One-Upmanship and God

The story of Jacob is the subject of most of the second half of the book of Genesis. At the outset it would be well for us to note the structure in which Genesis reproduces his biography. Broadly speaking, two episodes describe Jacob's relationship to his twin brother Esau, separated by another that depicts Jacob's experiences with Laban, his father-in-law. We may depict them as three panels hinged together by two major encounters between Jacob and God, one at the patriarch's exit from the Promised Land (Gen. 28:10-22), the other at his reentry into Canaan (chap. 32:24-32).

The announcement of Jacob's birth (chap. 25:21-23) and a confirmation of the change of the patriarch's name from Jacob to Israel, as well as a reaffirmation of the promises made to Abraham (chap. 35:9-12), enclose the three panels like an envelope. In the center of the middle panel we find the Lord's command to Jacob: " 'Go back to the land of your fathers and to your relatives, and I will be with you' " (chap. 31:3). The chart at the top of the next page will illustrate the pattern.

From a human perspective the stage was finally set for unimpeded success. Both the father and mother of God's elect had been carefully chosen. Isaac, the son of promise, had found a beautiful bride of acceptable

Divinely given birth oracle	Jacob and Esau	God meets Jacob at Bethel	Jacob	Divine command to return home	and Laban	God meets Jacob at Peniel	Jacob and Esau	Divine confirmation of change of names and blessing
Chap. 25:21-23		Chap. 28:10-22		Chap. 31:3, 13		Chap. 32:24-32		Chap. 35:5-12

stock. He was "forty years old when he married Rebekah daughter of Bethuel the Aramean from Paddan Aram and sister of Laban the Aramean" (chap. 25:20).

All too soon the couple discovered the tragic news that Rebekah was barren (verse 21). She suffered from the curse of sterility as had her deceased mother-in-law and as would her daughter-in-law Rachel. Once more the best of human arrangements and strategies had proved to be insufficient. Again it required a divine intervention, called for a miracle from God and trust in His grace and power. God would have to consummate the future and the promises in His own way.

"Isaac prayed to the Lord on behalf of his wife" (verse 21). For twenty years he had to bring his request before the Almighty, thus recognizing that life is a gift that cannot be forced (verse 26). John's words, though addressed to a somewhat different issue, apply equally to the children of Isaac, for Jacob and Esau were also "children born not . . . of human decision or a husband's will, but born of God" (John 1:13). In God's own time He answered Isaac's prayer, and "his wife . . . became pregnant" (Gen. 25:21). Clearly, the twins were solely a gift of grace and an answer to prayer.

Yet the gifts of God came in conflict. The record testifies to a prenatal sibling rivalry. "The babies jostled each other within her, and she said, 'Why is this happening to me?' So she went to inquire of the Lord. The Lord said to her, 'Two nations are in your womb, and two peoples from within you will be separated; one people will be stronger than the other, and the older will serve the younger'" (verses 22, 23). The struggle between the brothers first noticed by the puzzled pregnant mother-to-be came to expression again at the birth of the twins. At that time Jacob emerged, holding the heel of his brother as if to make one last effort to prevent Esau from being first (verse 26).

It hinted at the conflict that would ensue in later years, not only between the brothers but also between the two nations that would arise from Jacob and Esau. The Edomites, who descended from Esau, and the Israelites, whose ancestor was Jacob, though brother nations, became bitter enemies in later history.

In another sense the turmoil in Rebekah's womb foreshadowed the conflict that would characterize much of Jacob's life. The Lord's announcement " 'The older will serve the younger'" (verse 23) intimated and elicited the struggle.

It was customary in Old Testament times that the status of the firstborn was bound up with special privileges and prerogatives as well as with obligations and responsibilities. The tradition, called primogeniture, in patriarchal times conferred upon the oldest son precedence over his brothers and the right to the full inheritance of his father (e.g., verses 5, 6). Centuries later the eldest boy still obtained a double share of the inheritance and assumed the headship and priesthood of the family (see Deut. 21:17; compare Ex. 22:29 with Num. 8:14-17).

In the divine oracle the Lord inverted the customary roles played by the older and younger of the two brothers and transferred the birthright to Jacob. God is obviously free to carry out His will in spite of human conventions. The cultural presumptions of what is natural privilege could not restrict His power of choice. The transfer of the right of inheritance we also see sometime later in the cases of Reuben and Manasseh. Because Reuben committed a crime with his father's concubine Bilhah, Jacob deprived him of the privileges that naturally would have been his (Gen. 49:3, 4). Similarly, in blessing Joseph's two sons, Jacob passed over the older boy, Manasseh, in favor of his younger brother Ephraim (Gen. 48:13-20). We even have an example outside of Scripture from the extreme north-west of Syria in which those involved disregarded the rules of primogeniture.

Jacob's consciousness of his special status over that of his twin later led him to the heartless exploitation of his own brother and to the crafty deception practiced upon his blind old father (chapter 27). Such acts of duplicity brought in their train much of the conflict that dogged his steps throughout the remainder of his life.

In order to avoid the impression that Jacob's trickery had led to his preferred status, the Bible stresses that God chose him in preference to Esau. The election by the Lord, therefore, assumed a most important role in the context of the Jacob stories. The Bible carefully disengages Jacob's election from the improper means the patriarch used to secure for himself the right of the firstborn.

Scripture in no way condones Jacob's heartless schemes. It stresses that the younger of the twins had a claim to primogeniture solely by virtue of God's choice. Indeed, the divine oracle stating God's predetermina-tion and the story of Jacob's life are in effect a moral judgment on the patriarch's conduct. Several statements and stories implicitly condemn his unethical behavior. Thus, while the narrator stresses that Abraham and Isaac died at a good old age, "old and full of years" (chaps. 25:8 and 35:29), Jacob confesses before Pharaoh, "'My years have been few and difficult, and they do not equal the years of the pilgrimage of my fathers'" (chap. 47:9). While Jacob "was a quiet man, staying among the tents" (chap. 25:27), his duplicity caused him to leave home and hearth. The boy favored by his mother had to flee. His own mother's brother came to exploit the shrewd trickster. He who had disguised himself as his own brother and deceived his father in the darkness of failing eyesight was himself tricked into marrying a bride who masqueraded as her own sister and whose identity the darkness of night hid from him. The irony in the deception of Jacob consists of the fact that that which he had perpetrated on his father and brother in Canaan he in turn received from a sister and her father in Haran. Jacob outwitted his brother, father, and Laban; and Laban outsmarted Jacob. Both Jacob and Laban found a match in each other. Troubles for Jacob continued in Canaan. Upon his return, he feared his brother Esau, his only daughter was violated, beloved Rachel died in childbirth, and a son was sold into slavery. In a sense this sad biography of the patriarch itself condemns Jacob's schemes and trickery.

Both Isaac and Rebekah manifested preferential treatment for one of their boys. "Isaac, who had a taste for wild game, loved Esau, but Rebekah loved Jacob," who was a home-loving son (verses 27, 28). The tensions and feuds that developed between the two sets of family members culminated in the tragic scene described in Genesis 27.

Isaac's preference for his older boy blinded him to his son's follies and superficialities. In spite of the clear divine oracle that had invested Jacob with the birthright, the father was ready to confer blessings and obligations, upon Esau, which the older son had callously rejected. For a moment he resembled Esau, whose love for the immediate and the visible things in life far exceeded his desire for spiritual blessings. The father's natural desires became more important than moral and spiritual values. Isaac's reliance on his senses of taste, touch, and hearing, rather than on God's unmistakable wishes, proved his undoing and stands as a warning to those who depend solely upon empirical evidence for truth.

Rebekah's passionate devotion to Jacob led her to find a way by which the Lord's word " 'the older will serve the younger' " would not be thwarted through Isaac's stubborn plans. She was so determined that Jacob should have the birthright that she decided to use even wrong means to achieve the right ends. Rebekah loved Jacob more than truth, and placed happiness before honor. In contrast to her father-in-law, who had been ready to offer Isaac to truth and duty, she sacrificed duty to her son as she cajoled him into cooperation with her deceptive scheme. Jacob knew that if found out he would bring down upon himself a curse rather than a blessing (chap. 27:12). Yet his mother maintained, " 'My son, let the curse fall on me. Just do what I say' " (verse 13). Unwilling to trust God to right all wrongs, she offered to take upon herself the retribution that her son feared. However, instead of blessing, she only caused her son's downfall.

Once Jacob consented to Rebekah's strategy, he soon became entangled in an ever-tightening web of sin. Masquerading as Esau, he first lied to his father, " 'I am Esau your first born. I have done as you told me. Please sit up and eat'" (verse 19). The puzzled and doubtful father asked, "'Are you really my son Esau?'" Jacob, unwilling to escape the grasp of sin and deception, answered "'I am'" (verse 24).

The trickster was even prepared to implicate God in his scheme. When surprised by the speedy compliance to his request for game, Isaac questioned, "'How did you find it so quickly, my son?'" Jacob responded, "'The Lord your God gave me success'" (verse 20). "From the hour when he received the birthright, Jacob was weighed down with self-condemnation. He had sinned against his father, his brother, his own soul, and against God. In one short hour he had made work for a lifelong repentance. This scene was vivid before him in afteryears, when the wicked course of his own sons oppressed his soul."[35]

While Jacob subsequently repented of his sin and received forgiveness, Esau regretted only the loss of his privilege. He cared primarily for the immediate gratification of his desires and manifested little interest in the more significant rights and responsibilities bound up with the birthright. Nothing mattered more to the famished hunter returning from the open country than a pot of lentils. Primogeniture and its attendant blessings were of less value to the brash and indifferent man than the present satisfaction of his senses.

Imprudently Esau remarked when Jacob bartered for the right of inheritance, "'What good is the birthright to me?'" (chap. 25:32). Neither qualms nor remorse seemed to bother the older brother. Instead he confirmed his sad choice with a solemn oath (verse 33). Esau's lack of concern over the surrender of the birthright he further demonstrated by his untroubled departure. The record simply says, "He ate and drank, and then got up and left. So Esau despised his birthright" (verse 34). "In disposing of . . . [the right of inheritance] he felt a sense of relief. Now his way was unobstructed; he could do as he liked. For this wild pleasure, miscalled freedom, how many are still selling their birthright to an inheritance pure and undefiled, eternal in the heavens!" [36]

When Esau finally realized that he had lost the birthright forever, he broke down in remorse and tears (chap. 27:33-38). Though Esau complained to his father that he had been cheated twice, implying his own innocence, he was not telling the truth. The heartbroken man moves one with pity, yet we must put his regret into proper perspective. Scripture says, "See that no one is . . . godless like Esau, who for a single meal sold his inheritance rights as the oldest son. Afterward, as you know, when he wanted to inherit this blessing, he was rejected. He could bring about no change of mind, though he sought the blessing with tears" (Heb. 12:16, 17).

Esau showed a similar independence of spirit in his marriages to several Hittite girls. He revealed an indifference to the feelings and ideals of his parents and family as he united with unbelieving women who proved to be "a source of grief to Isaac and Rebekah" (Gen. 26:35; compare chaps. 27:46; 28:6, 7). His conduct demonstrates his father's folly in ignoring the divine oracle as he sought to bestow upon his son the blessing of the elect. While we can only disapprove of Jacob's exploitation of both his brother and father, we have to acknowledge the ultimate wisdom of God's choice of Jacob as the heir to the sacred covenant privileges.

All four participants in this episode had done wrong. Isaac attempted to thwart God's election. Esau had no right to seek the privileges that he had bartered

away under oath. Jacob and Rebekah stood condemned of their conduct and their inability to trust
God to accomplish His own purposes.

Strangely, the very blessing that had been intended
for good became a source for anxiety and made the
younger of the twins a fugitive. The bounty that the
cunning schemer tried to wrest from his brother
turned into a burden. God's gracious blessings
obviously had their own way. Ultimately both failures
and deceptions had to conform to God's overriding
providential purpose, which utilized both human
strengths and weaknesses.

Once again Rebekah began to scheme. In the face of
threats from Esau to take revenge, she realized that she
would have to lose her son to save him. Calling Jacob to
her, she advised, " 'Your brother Esau is consoling
himself with the thought of killing you. Now then, my
son, do what I say: Flee at once to my brother Laban in
Haran. Stay with him for a while. . . . When your brother
is no longer angry with you and forgets what you did to
him, I'll send word for you to come back from there' "
(chap. 27:42-45). In her fear and unwillingness to trust
the Lord, she mingled truth and ruse in order to win
Isaac's approval for Jacob's journey to her ancestral
home. What Rebekah did not know then was that she
would never see her son again on this earth.

The interactions between the various members of
the family described in chapter 27 give way to a direct
confrontation between the fugitive and God (chapter
28). Jacob, guilty and burdened with sin, and full of
remorse, had fallen asleep near the village later known
as Bethel. Only divine grace initiated the encounter
between God and Jacob. Though the wanderer did not
deserve the vision of God, he desperately needed it.

It is significant that in the dream at Bethel the Lord

did not review Jacob's shameful past. Notwithstanding his previous sin, God assured the distressed fugitive that heaven had not abandoned him to his own resources. The Lord portrayed His care through the symbol of the stairway that the tired man saw "resting on the earth, with its top reaching to heaven, and the angels of God were ascending and descending on it" (chap. 28:12). Above the stairway stood the Lord, identifying Himself as the God of Jacob's forefathers. Heaven was no longer remote from the earth. The surprise element in the whole episode consists in the fact that God would actually appear to the treacherous runaway.

The Lord knew that Jacob was not satisfied merely with the material benefits of the birthright and that he anxiously longed also for the spiritual blessings. For this reason God reiterated and extended the earlier promises, saying, " 'I will give you and your descendants the land on which you are lying. Your descendants will be like the dust of the earth, and you will spread out to the west and to the east, to the north and to the south. All peoples on earth will be blessed through you and your offspring' " (verses 13, 14).

In addition, He informed the travel-worn and lonely sleeper longing for reassurance, " 'I am with you and will watch over you wherever you go, and I will bring you back to this land. I will not leave you until I have done what I have promised you' " (verse 15). Overcome by a sense of gratitude and wonder at the revelation of divine patience, love, and forgiveness, Jacob made a vow and surrendered himself and his possessions in an act of commitment to the Lord (verses 20-22). With the Lord and His word by his side, Jacob could face the future, whatever might come.

From Bethel to Peniel

With Jacob's departure to Bethel and arrival in Haran, the Jacob-Laban episode commences (Genesis 29). The entry of Jacob at Haran differed markedly from the arrival of Eliezer some ninety-seven years before. Whereas ten camels richly laden with "all kinds of good things from his master" accompanied Eliezer, Jacob arrived poor and on foot (compare chaps. 24:10 and 29:1-13). On both occasions, Laban extended typical Eastern hospitality to the visitors, though it seems that the sight of the jewelry that Eliezer had given to Rebekah hastened his steps and added eloquence to the welcome extended to Abraham's servant (chap. 24:30, 31). Nevertheless, the invitation given to Jacob, who poured out the sad story of his past, was equally sincere (chap. 29:13, 14).

After Jacob had worked for one month on Laban's property, his uncle recognized the financial advantage to him should he retain his nephew's services (verses 14, 15). As Genesis does not mention any sons until a much later period, he may have intended to adopt Jacob as the heir to his property in conformity with ancient Near Eastern custom. All too soon, however, Jacob discovered that in his uncle he had met a trickster who was every bit his equal, and much of the ensuing story becomes a commentary on the principle that "a man reaps what he sows" (Gal. 6:7).

Soon after Jacob agreed to work for seven years in exchange for Laban's younger daughter—a deal acceptable to both suitor and prospective father-in-law—he met his first heartrending disappointment in Mesopotamia. Under the pretense that the older child should have precedence over the younger, Laban gave to him Leah, the older daughter masquerading as her younger sister. The patriarch, who in the past had wrestled with this same convention and had tried to gain preeminence over his older brother, experienced the bitter disappointment Esau must have felt when the older brother forever lost the birthright. Incensed by the ruse, Jacob accused Laban of deception and learned firsthand how cruel it can be (Gen. 29:25, 26; compare chap. 27:36). In order to obtain the hand of the girl he passionately loved, the septuagenerian agreed to labor for another seven years, a proposal that Laban had greedily suggested (compare verses 20, 27-30).

Though Rachel "was lovely in form, and beautiful" she was also petulent and selfish. Like Sarah and Rebekah before her, she suffered from the curse of barrenness. In a society in which childlessness brought shame and humiliation, Rachel became jealous of her sister, who had already given four sons to Jacob. Impatiently she demanded of Jacob, "'Give me children, or I'll die!'" (chap. 30:1). A family, or clan, required children—particularly sons—for both its strength and maintenance. Lacking trust in God, she suggested to her husband that he sleep with Bilhah, her maidservant (verse 3).

When sometime later Leah's oldest boy Reuben went out into the field during the time of the wheat harvest and found some mandrake plants, which he brought to his mother, "Rachel said to Leah, 'Please give me some of your son's mandrakes'" (verse 14). Since, according to superstition, mandrakes stimulated sexual desire and promoted fertility, Leah responded angrily to her sister's selfishness, "'Wasn't it enough that you took away my husband? Will you take my son's mandrakes too?'" (verse 15). Curiously, the mandrakes that Leah finally surrendered to Rachel in exchange for the privilege of sexual intimacy with Jacob proved ineffective. It was Leah, instead of the desperate and grasping Rachel, who fell pregnant.

Rachel appears also to have been less committed spiritually than Leah. Not only do we see it demonstrated in her lack of faith in God as evidenced in her attempts to secure children through Bilhah, but also in her continued attachment to her father's gods. Rachel's devotion to the deities was so pronounced that she decided to steal them when the caravan of Jacob fled from Haran (chap. 31:19). Nevertheless, we also have occasional positive glimpses of her. Frustrated by her schemes to cast off her sterility, she fled to God, and once again God *remembered.* In answer to her petition the Lord enabled her to give birth to Joseph (whose name means "may he add"); and then she pleaded, "'May the Lord add to me another son'" (chap. 30:24).

Although Leah came from the same semipagan background and manifested weaknesses of faith like Rachel by resorting to concubinage in order to secure children, she revealed a deeper commitment to the God of Jacob. Three of her first four children received names that invoked that of the "Lord," suggesting that she had accepted the God her spouse worshiped. Though deceitful at first and physically less attractive than her younger sister, Leah gathers our sympathy to herself. She never featured in a primary role in Jacob's life, yet always remained loyal to him. Indeed, the fact that Jacob buried Leah in the ancestral cave-sepulchre may indicate that his affection for her had gradually developed.

After fourteen years of service, at the end of which Joseph appears to have been born, Jacob requested Laban's blessing to return to his homeland (chap. 30:22-25). Reticent to lose such a valuable worker, Laban wanted him to stay on. So when Jacob proposed a deal by which he might gather some assets for himself, the uncle readily agreed. " 'Let me go through all your flocks today and remove from them every speckled or spotted sheep, every dark-colored lamb and every spotted or speckled goat,' " Jacob suggested. " 'They will be my wages' " (verse 32). Given the fact that in the Middle East only a small portion of flocks and herds would consist of off-color sheep and goats, selfish Laban would normally have been left with the largest part of the flock.

Immediately Laban separated the off-color animals to prevent the chance of having their characteristics bred back into what appeared pure-colored stock. The sequel to the episode reveals that neither of the men was aware of the fact that even the pure-colored sheep and goats carried recessive color characteristics that they could pass on to their offspring. The Lord blessed Jacob in his work for his father-in-law, and in spite of his clever but ineffective strategies and schemes, increased the patriarch's wealth.

Greed, avarice, and meanness characterized much of Laban. He cared primarily for his own advancement, and in the process he disregarded the feelings of his daughters and their husband. Though he quickly agreed to Jacob's terms of service, he was ready to forget the ending of the period and the promised wages (chap. 29:21). On his flight from Haran, Jacob confronted his pursuing father-in-law and accused him: " 'I have been with you for twenty years now. . . . I did not bring you animals torn by wild beasts; I bore the loss myself. And you demanded payment from me for whatever was stolen by day or by night. . . . I worked for you fourteen years for your two daughters and six years for your flocks, and you changed my wages ten times. If the God of my father, the God of Abraham and the Fear of Isaac, had not been with me, you would surely have sent me away empty-handed' " (chap. 31:38-42).

Laban's selfishness and cruel mercenary spirit alienated him not only from Jacob but also from his daughters and their children. Both Leah and Rachel advised their husband, " 'Do we still have any share in the inheritance of our father's estate? Does he not regard us as foreigners? Not only has he sold us, but he has used up what was paid for us' " (verse 14).

The increasing hostility and antagonism between Laban and Jacob finally provided the occasion for the patriarch's return. Once more the God of Bethel appeared to Jacob and ordered, " 'Now leave this land at once and go back to your native land' " (verse 13). Following Jacob's departure for Canaan, the contacts between the family members in Mesopotamia and Palestine ceased, and the Jacob-Laban episode came to an end.

Thoroughly disciplined by his father-in-law's activity, Jacob longed to return to his homeland. However, before returning to the "house of God" (Bethel) to bring the promised offering, he sought reconciliation with his brother. We may compare Jacob's action on this journey with the principles Jesus laid out in the Sermon on the Mount. When dealing with an aggrieved party, He advised, " 'If you are offering your gift at the altar and there remember that your brother has something against you, leave the gift there in front of the altar. First go and be reconciled to your brother; then come and offer your gift' " (Matt. 5:23, 24).

Burdened with the guilt of deceiving his father and brother, Jacob felt greatly relieved when God sent His angels to protect the caravan. As he saw the angelic host he exclaimed, " 'This is the camp of God!' " (Gen. 32:2). The patriarch memorialized the event by naming the location at which the angels of God met him Mahanaim (meaning "two camps"). In order to bring about reconciliation with his brother, Jacob sent messengers to Esau, who had left Beersheba and now resided "in the land of Seir, the country of Edom" (verses 3-5). The message they carried was designed to disarm Esau in case he still bore hostility against his twin brother. Hence Jacob addressed Esau as " 'my master' " and " 'my lord' " while he identified himself as " 'your servant Jacob' " (verse 4, 5, 18). Furthermore, the patriarch stated that he had accumulated sufficient wealth in his cattle, donkeys, sheep, and goats, menservants and maidservants, and thus assured Esau that he had not returned to claim his paternal inheritance.

When news reached the company that Esau was coming with four hundred men, fear and distress seized everyone. The patriarch immediately laid plans to meet the emergency. He divided the camp into two groups to preserve at least one half should an attack destroy the other (verses 7, 8). Then Jacob selected and sent presents of some 550 head of goats, sheep, cattle, donkeys, and camels to pacify his brother (verses 13-20). Once he had attended to all that he could humanly do to face the impending danger, Jacob resorted to prayer and left the rest in the hands of God.

In his petition the patriarch acknowledged his own unworthiness of the divine kindness and faithfulness shown and claimed God's love and care in the past as the only grounds for his present petition (verse 10). After all, Jacob recalled both at the beginning and end of his prayer, his present errand was in accord with God's specific command (verses 9 and 12). He observed that were Esau to destroy the group, then it would threaten the success of the divinely ordained mission. While recognizing our own unworthiness, it is still our privilege today to throw ourselves upon the mercy of God and to claim His promises. The Lord honored his trust.

By nightfall the whole company had forded the Jabbok. The excitement of the day, with its noise of a large traveling caravan, had passed, and Jacob stood alone before God in the silence of night. Once more old memories awakened. Conscience became active, and former fears revived. Like most of us, Jacob was a complex person. He had some of his grandfather's deep faith and some of his father's loyalty. At the same time he also possessed some of his grandmother's jealousy and his mother's shrewdness and unscrupulousness. However, we cannot simply hold genes and chromosomes or environment responsible for what we are. More important is the recognition that we are the product of our own choices. The values and ideals we elect and the traits we promote in ourselves are ultimately of greatest significance. Similarly, by God's grace Jacob could reject his past life and the image represented by his name Jacob ("deceiver" or "heel catcher").

As he stood by the brook, still wrestling with remorse, guilt, and doubt, he had an unforgettable experience. A stranger attacked him. Little by little, the patriarch perceived that the intruder was none other than God, a recognition the patriarch memorialized in the place name Peniel (meaning "face of God") (verse 30; compare Hosea 12:3, 4). As Jacob became aware of the identity of the person with whom he struggled he pleaded earnestly for the well-being that he had sought so long (verses 26, 29). God granted his wish in the form of a change of his name and of a blessing. The heavenly visitor informed the patriarch, " 'Your name will no longer be Jacob, but Israel ["he struggles with God"], because you have struggled with God and with men and have overcome' " (verse 28). God now elevated to honor the man whose name once spelled discredit.

As Jacob stepped out of the darkness into the sunrise he had a more intimate knowledge of God and an impediment that would never let him forget the experience at Peniel. At Bethel he had experienced God at the top of a stairway, but at Peniel he had met Him face to face. Subsequent history reveals that the lame Israel was a better person than the spritely Jacob. Often the pains we endure make us better and more understanding people. Though with his hip out of joint he appeared shorter outwardly, he had grown taller within.

The encounter with God enabled him to reenter the Land of Promise as a man of faith. Although he had feared the meeting with Esau, his concerns proved to be unnecessary. When Esau saw his brother he "ran to meet Jacob and embraced him; he threw his arms around his neck and kissed him. And they wept" (chap. 33:4).

Magnanimously Esau offered to accompany the caravan, but Jacob declined him. Trusting in the Lord's promised protection, he thought of the needs of both his children and livestock. He reminded Esau, " 'My lord knows that the children are tender and that I must care for the ewes and cows that are nursing their young. . . . So let my lord go on ahead of his servant, while I move along slowly at the pace of the droves before me and that of the children, until I come to my lord in Seir' " (verses 13, 14).

While Jacob's concern for the welfare of his dependants is exemplary, his comment about meeting his brother in Seir puzzles us. Why did he not inform Esau that he was under oath to travel to Bethel? At best his statement expressed some future intention that as far as the record goes, never materialized, while at worst it reflected some of Jacob's previous deviousness. Clearly Jacob decided to go neither to Bethel nor to Seir. Instead, he settled east of the Jordan at Succoth, "where he built a place for himself and made shelters for his livestock" (verse 17). After his only daughter Dinah had grown into womanhood he moved to Shechem, still about a day's journey short of Bethel.

During Jacob's sojourn at Shechem tragedy hit with a vengeance. Dinah, who visited the women of Shechem, was raped, and her brothers treacherously massacred the Shechemites in revenge (chapter 34). The events at Shechem were largely the result of Jacob's tardiness in following God's call to Bethel. The chapter reflects life in the raw and traces for us the lustful passions of the local prince, the pathos of the young raped Dinah, and the brutality of the brothers' revenge. Jacob's sons had judged Shechem's action as "a thing that should not be done" (verse 7), yet their own massacre violated both moral conscience and the law of exact retribution for a crime. They condemned Shechem's rape as "a disgraceful thing in Israel" (verse 7), while their own vile cruelty exceeded the crime of the pagan prince. Their schemes consisted of foul deceit, cold-blooded treachery, and pitiless slaughter. They demeaned the covenant sign of circumcision and passed off their cruel violence as alleged administration of justice. How different it all might have been had Jacob been faithful to God and his own promise, and gone on to Bethel!

Once more God instructed him, " 'Go up to Bethel and settle there, and build an altar there to God, who appeared to you when you were fleeing from your brother Esau' " (chap. 35:1; compare chap. 31:3, 13). The Lord led the patriarch right back to the very place where he had first met him many years before. In the light of his and his family's recent failures, Jacob called the whole group to revival and reformation. The family purified itself and surrendered the images and orna-ments, which he buried at Shechem. At Bethel Jacob erected an altar in memory of the God who had fulfilled His promises to him and once more received the promises given to his forefathers. Here the most significant part of Jacob's career began and ended. From now on, his older son to Rachel, Joseph, will become the focus of the remaining chapters of the book of Genesis.

"You Sold . . .
God Sent"

Genesis 37-41 describes the first thirty years of Joseph's life. These chapters organize its material around *three* sets of *double dreams*. In the *first* of them Joseph saw himself and his family binding sheaves of grain in the field, when suddenly his sheaf rose and stood upright, while those of his family gathered around Joseph's and bowed down to it (chap. 37:6, 7). Later Joseph had another dream; "'this time the sun and moon and eleven stars were bowing down'" to him (verses 9, 10). The two dreams generated considerable hatred and contributed significantly to his sale into Egypt, as is clear from the reaction of Jacob's sons when they saw him approach them near Dothan. They said, "'Here comes that dreamer! . . . Come now, let's kill him and throw him into one of these cisterns and say that a ferocious animal devoured him. Then we'll see what becomes of his dreams'" (verses 19, 20).

Instead of letting him perish in the cistern, however, they sold Joseph to a group of traders on their way to Egypt. Once in Egypt, he found himself cruelly rewarded for his integrity and thrown into jail. Here the young man faced *another* set of double dreams, which came to Pharaoh's cupbearer and baker. The cupbearer had seen a three-branched vine, which had budded, blossomed, and ripened into clusters of grapes. He took and squeezed them into Pharaoh's cup, which the cupbearer had in his hand (chap. 40:9-11). The baker dreamed that he had carried three baskets of bread on his head. The uppermost basket contained all kinds of baked goods intended for the Pharaoh, but which birds consumed (verses 16, 17).

The fulfillment of Joseph's interpretation of the cupbearer's dream specifying his release from jail and restitution to the court ultimately led to the Hebrew slave's introduction to the Egyptian court on the occasion of a double dream by Pharaoh himself. The ruler had seen seven sleek and fat cows, which seven ugly and gaunt ones consumed. Another dream soon followed. In it seven heads of thin and scorched grain swallowed up seven heads of healthy and good grain (chap. 41:2-7).

Joseph's successful interpretation of the *third* set of double dreams led to the coming true of his own dream given to him some thirteen years earlier. Elevated to rulership in Egypt, he received obeisance from his brothers when they arrived in Egypt to purchase grain for the survival of their family (chap. 42:6, 8, 9). Thus the three sets of double dreams form the thread that links these initial thirteen years of Joseph. During these years he experienced harsh cruelties, savage servitude, and finally elevation to the prime ministership of Egypt. The three sets of double dreams linking chapters 37-41 the chart on the next page will illustrate.

Joseph was the older son of Jacob's favored wife, Rachel, born when his father was 91 years of age. Since Rachel had died near Ephrath, which scholars believe was Bethlehem, while giving birth to Benjamin, Jacob had become both father and mother to his son. It is not unlikely that Joseph closely resembled his mother in

Joseph's dreams of	Royal officers' dreams of	Pharaoh's dreams of
1. sheaves	1. grapes	1. cows
2. heavenly bodies	2. bread	2. grain

appearance, and for that reason reminded the father of his beloved Rachel (compare chaps. 29:17; 39:6). This resemblance may explain why Jacob appears to have transferred the affections he would have showered upon his late wife to the boy.

From the outset the narrator states that enmity existed between Joseph and his brothers. The mounting hatred between them resulted from a series of events (chap. 37:4, 5, 8). First, Joseph had brought a bad report about the evil conduct of his brothers Dan, Naphtali, Gad, and Asher (verse 2; compare chap. 30:4-12). Second, the Bible records that "Israel loved Joseph more than any of his other sons, because he had been born to him in his old age; and he made a richly ornamented robe for him" (verse 3). Obviously Jacob had learned little from the mistake of his parents, particularly his mother, who had shown preferential treatment for him and caused both of them much pain in after years (compare chap. 25:28). Now the patriarch demonstrated the favoritism by the special robe that he made for Joseph. Although the precise meaning of the Hebrew word describing the robe is uncertain, the phrase appears to designate a coat extending to the floor with long sleeves. Translations following the Greek version of the Old Testament suggest that it was a multicolored coat. Whatever the exact nature of the garment, it distinguished him from his brothers. Jacob's partiality for Joseph increased the hostility the other sons felt toward their brother and contributed directly to the grief Jacob would experience later.

Third, Joseph's narration of his dreams, which

clearly implied his supremacy over the rest of the family, intensified his brothers' resentment and hatred (chap. 37:5-11). The fact that he recounted his second dream despite the growing awareness of his family's negative reaction to him reveals his immaturity. Jacob may have intended his rebuke to correct this (verses 10, 11).

The hatred of Jacob's sons culminated in the decision to dispose of their brother permanently. Only the arrival of a caravan of Ishmaelites saved him from certain death in a cistern. Betrayed by his own brothers for the mere pittance of twenty shekels of silver, the 17-year-old went to Egypt as a lonely slave (verse 28). Why did God permit such cruelty and injustice? Apart from his adolescent lack of judgment, Joseph had done nothing deserving of such cruelty. The events must have seemed as inexplicable to Joseph as they appear to us.

Once in Egypt, the slave traders sold Joseph to Potiphar, "one of Pharaoh's officials, the captain of the guard" (verse 36). Genesis draws attention to the fact that Potiphar was an *Egyptian* (chap. 39:1). Since to mention this detail appears rather strange, scholars have suggested that a non-Egyptian dynasty may have ruled the region of the Nile at that time. The rulers that best fit the hints provided by the book of Genesis are the Hyksos, Asiatics who dominated Egypt between approximately 1780 and 1550 B.C.

Spliced between the story of Joseph's sale to Potiphar and the account of his service in the home of the captain of the guard is an interlude reporting about Judah's family and his relationships to his daughter-in-law Tamar (chapter 38). Judah was both an older brother of Joseph and the instigator of the plan to sell him to the Ishmaelites (chap. 37:26, 27). The chapter describes Judah's departure from his brothers and his walk "down to stay with a man of Adullam" (chap. 38:1). Tragically, he had gone *down* both geographically and spiritually and entered into an intimate and unholy alliance with the Canaanites. From his marriage to the daughter of a Canaanite man named Shua issued three sons.

The first boy, married to Tamar, "was wicked in the Lord's sight; so the Lord put him to death" (verse 7). The second son, who by a custom called levirate marriage (from the Latin *levir*, "brother-in-law") was obligated to marry his sister-in-law in order to maintain his brother's family, spurned Tamar, and because of his wickedness also perished (verses 8-10). Pretending that he would give Tamar his youngest boy as soon as he reached adulthood in order to fulfill the levirate marriage obligation, Judah sent his daughter-in-law to her father's house.

Since it became apparent to Tamar that Judah had no intentions of keeping his promise, she decided to secure a child through her father-in-law. The remainder of the chapter describes Judah's surrender to lust with his own daughter-in-law, who had disguised herself as a cult prostitute. Genesis 38 contrasts the lack of integrity of the betrayer Judah and the moral excellence of the betrayed Joseph. On one hand we read of Judah's profligacy in Canaan; on the other, we will admire Joseph's moral integrity in Egypt.

The next chapter returns the reader to the sale of Joseph and focuses on his life in Egypt. Bought by Potiphar and put to work in his house, Pharaoh's official soon discovered that success attended all the Hebrew slave did. Because of his willingness to apply himself to the duties laid upon him, the Lord honored Joseph with singular success. Before long Potiphar appointed the young man steward of his household, and "the blessing of the Lord was on everything Potiphar had, both in the house and in the field. So he left in Joseph's care everything he had; with Joseph in charge, he did not concern himself with anything except the food he ate" (chap. 39:5, 6).

Joseph's response to Potiphar's wife reveals his intimate relationship with God and testifies to his inner moral strength. The exile saw the privileges his master had bestowed upon him as a reason for loyalty. He responded to his seductress, " 'With me in charge, . . . my master does not concern himself with anything in the house; everything he owns he has entrusted to my care. No one is greater in his house than I am. My master has withheld nothing from me except you, because you are his wife. How then could I do such a wicked thing and sin against God?' " (verses 8, 9).

His reverence for God and moral fiber enabled him to recognize the wife's sensuality and resist. While a weaker man may have argued, "How can I not do it?" Joseph stated resolutely, " 'How then could I do such a wicked thing?' " The young man sensed God's continuous presence and recognized that ultimately all sin touches God. He recognized that in the final analysis we demonstrate character by what a person is and does in the dark. Joseph's success corroborates the truthfulness of Paul's words "I can do everything through him who gives me strength" (Phil. 4:13).

For the second time Joseph's coat nearly led to his death! Once more he received a cruel reward for his faithfulness to duty and integrity as his resolute stand resulted in imprisonment. There the psalmist states, "They bruised his feet with shackles," and "his neck was put in irons" (Ps. 105:18). Such unfairness appalls our sense of moral justice. Had Joseph cursed God and man, we would almost excuse him. However, the captive became neither morose nor distrustful. He was conscious of his innocence and trusted his case with God. As prisoner, Joseph threw himself into the work assigned to him. Endeavoring to lighten the heartaches of others, he was able to bear, and even forget, his own sorrows. Once more the success attending his labor did not go unnoticed, and he was put "in charge of all those held in the prison, and he was made responsible for all that was done there" (Gen. 39:22).

Sometime after his imprisonment the warden assigned him to serve two royal officials placed in custody presumably for suspected disloyalty. One was the royal cupbearer; the other the king's baker. Both had dreams that predicted their own future, and Joseph interpreted them. The dream of the chief cupbearer implied a favorable outcome, and Pharaoh had him released soon thereafter. The dream of the baker predicted his execution, which occurred three days later.

Joseph had been so certain of the fulfillment of the dreams of the two high-ranking court officials that he requested the cupbearer, " 'When all goes well with you, remember me and show me kindness; mention me to Pharaoh and get me out of this prison. For I was forcibly carried off from the land of the Hebrews, and even here I have done nothing to deserve being put in a dungeon' " (chap. 40:14, 15).

With the vindication of the butler, Joseph expected his own release. We do not know what thoughts crossed his mind as days, weeks, and months passed without a sign of deliverance. How shattering must have been the realization that the official had forgotten him. Scripture describes the tragedy briefly. "The chief cupbearer, however, did not remember Joseph; he forgot him" (verse 23). Once more, Joseph's experience brings protest to one's lips. Was it not enough that the betrayal of his own brothers had hurt him? Had he not been wounded sufficiently by a woman's passion turned to anger? Why another injury?

While the butler did not attack him as directly or deliberately as had his brothers or Potiphar's wife, he bruised him simply by doing nothing. Indeed, sins of omission are at times more painful than ones of commission. How often our best intentions and promises wither like poorly rooted or unwatered flowers, and we find ourselves led to confess, "We have left undone those things that we ought to have done."

Once more we find ourselves asking, "Why did God permit such injustice and injury?" Had He become indifferent to one of His servants? Had the Lord been outwitted in the administration of His affairs?

While Scripture is sparing in its responses to most of our queries, its answers far outweigh the significance of our questions. Joseph resolved his problems in the recognition of God's overruling providence. When sometime later he revealed his identity to his brothers, he told the terrified men, *"You sold [me],"* but *"God sent me"* (chap. 45:4, 7). The prime minister of Egypt had recognized *two sides to life.* He was sufficiently realistic not to deny the cruelty, hatred, pain, questioning, and discouragement he had experienced.

Yet beyond this, Joseph discerned another side. As he faced his brothers in all their need, the eyes of faith discovered God's purpose superseding the best of man-laid plans. He clearly recognized that no amount of evil intentions can defeat the divine plan—rather, such wicked plans become ways by which God furthers His purposes. The Lord had sent the young man ahead to Egypt to save their lives, and no human schemes could frustrate His intentions.

Though Joseph is the protagonist in the account beginning with Genesis 37, God is really the hero in the story. The Bible seeks to teach us that God's plan succeeds in spite of the failings of both those on His side and of those who attempt to oppose His purposes. Through the jealousies and hatreds of Joseph's brothers God set the scene for the descent of Jacob and his family into Egypt (chaps. 15: 13-16; 46).

Harmony and Hope

Famine and hunger struck Canaan once again. When Jacob learned that grain was available in Egypt, he told his sons, "'I have heard that there is grain in Egypt. Go down there and buy some for us, so that we may live and not die'" (Gen. 42:2). In response, ten of the brothers traveled southwest and soon found themselves before Joseph, the prime minister of Egypt.

When his brothers arrived, "they bowed down to him with their faces to the ground. As soon as Joseph saw his brothers, he recognized them, but he pretended to be a stranger" (verses 6, 7). More than two decades had passed since they had sold Joseph into slavery. Because he occupied the highest office of the land, the sons of Jacob never suspected the governor to be their brother. As they bowed low before him Joseph recalled the dreams about them twenty years ago. While these same men had tried to prevent their fulfillment, they had actually unwittingly advanced them. Joseph's rule over his brothers was a consequence of his authority over Egypt. Now the unique opportunity to take revenge for all their cruelty had come, but he rose above personal injury and prejudice.

Nevertheless, the absence of Benjamin seems to have aroused the governor's suspicions. Had they also conveniently eliminated his younger brother? Joseph was determined to discover the truth about Benjamin, his father, and his family. Resorting to a ruse, he singled out the ten men from among the crowd and accused them of being undercover agents who had come to Egypt to gather intelligence (verses 9-12). Desert tribes were always trying to invade the fertile land of the Nile. In their defense the brothers revealed some of the family history, the truthfulness of which Joseph determined to test. Having detained them for three days, Joseph summoned the men to go to Canaan with grain for their starving families and return with their youngest brother. But he kept Simeon in Egypt as hostage.

The fright, horror, and peril of their experience made such a deep impression upon the brothers that it reminded them of Joseph's sale years before. They sensed that their distress and anguish paralleled that of the abandoned and brutally treated younger brother. The conviction that God was judging them for their ancient guilt overwhelmed them completely. They said to one another, "'Surely we are being punished because of our brother. We saw how distressed he was when he pleaded with us for his life, but we would not listen; that's why this distress has come upon us'" (verse 21).

The men were convinced that the calamity was nothing but a punishment for their inhumanity to Joseph. The knowledge of their wrongdoing had followed them like shadows throughout the years and deprived them of the peace of innocence. Once more they discovered that buried guilt will not remain concealed. The brothers' anguish intensified when upon their return journey they discovered in each man's sack the purchase money for the grain. "Their hearts sank, and they turned to each other trembling and said, 'What is this that *God* has done to us?' " (verse 28).

Jacob's refusal to let the men return with Benjamin delayed their journey to Egypt (verses 36-38). Even though their father was not aware of the hidden crime against Joseph, he knew their characters only too well to entrust them with his beloved youngest son. Their treacherous massacre of the Shechemites (chapter 34) did not invite his confidence. Reuben's suggestion " 'You may put both of my sons to death if I do not bring him [i.e., Benjamin] back to you. Entrust him to my care, and I will bring him back' " (chap. 42:37) was as impetuous as had been his heinous sin of lying with his father's concubine Bilhah (chap. 35:22). How would the slaughter of Reuben's two boys compensate for the loss of Benjamin? All the old father could see were two lost sons and the possible loss of another (verse 36).

However, the force of the unabating famine conditions and the rapidly declining food supply, as well as the repeated entreaties of his sons, finally persuaded Jacob to release Benjamin and his brothers for their second journey to Egypt (chap. 43:1-15). Upon reaching their destination, the brothers presented themselves before Joseph, who instructed his steward to entertain them at his home (verses 16-25). The sons of Jacob were terrified, for they surmised that the invitation was merely a pretext to seize them and their goods " 'because of the silver that was put back into our sacks the first time' " (verse 18). The steward, whom Joseph had probably taken into his confidence and who had accepted his ruler's God as his own, tried to allay their fears with words of kindness and acts of unusual hospitality (verses 23, 24).

When Joseph arrived at his residence, the brothers hoped to placate him by presenting to him gifts (verses

25, 26). After accepting their obeisance once again, the prime minister inquired about the welfare of their aged father and showed unusual kindness to Benjamin (verses 26-30). Clearly, Benjamin was still alive, but what of the brothers' attitude toward him? Did the men feel the same hostility to Benjamin as they had displayed to Joseph? In order to test them, he decided to show partiality to the younger brother at the meal. The lack of resentment toward Benjamin, who now occupied a special place in his father's heart, demonstrated that a transformation had occurred in the hearts of his brothers (verses 33, 34).

However, Joseph determined to apply one more crucial and final test in order to appraise fully the attitude of Jacob's sons toward both their father and youngest brother. He placed the men in a situation similar to that when they had cruelly sold him. Would their personal concerns and considerations once more outweigh love for father and brother? Would a reenactment of the former situation issue in another betrayal? Previously the reward for the betrayal had been twenty pieces of silver—now it would be their own freedom.

The instrument for the test was to be Joseph's silver goblet, which he had placed in Benjamin's grain sack (chap. 44:1, 2). Unsuspectingly the eleven men set out for Canaan. They had not traveled far when Joseph's steward intercepted them and accused them of stealing the cup (verses 3-6). Frightened, they protested their innocence and proposed, " 'If any of your servants is found to have it [i.e., the silver cup], he will die; and the rest of us will become my lord's slaves' " (verse 9). Seeking to demonstrate their innocence, the men responded impetuously and injudiciously, particularly in the light of the mysterious appearance of the purchase money in their sacks on their first return to Canaan. In their agitation they fully committed the guilty to death and the rest to slavery.

However, the steward graciously commuted the proposed death sentence to lifelong slavery and released the other brothers from blame (verse 10). The search began with the oldest and ended with the youngest, the very same order in which the servants had seated them at the feast in the prime minister's house. Though the brothers had been astonished on the earlier occasion, no suspicions were aroused this time. The Scripture passes over the suspense and drama of the search. The increasing relief and possible expressions of annoyance at the harassment as the Egyptians opened sack after sack turned into abject despair and terror as the goblet surfaced in Benjamin's sack (verses 12, 13). He stood condemned to a life of slavery. Would the sons of Jacob once again betray a brother and break a father's heart?

Returning to the city, the men prostrated themselves before Joseph. Judah, who had suggested Joseph's sale to the Ishmaelites, now pleaded on behalf of Benjamin (verses 16-34; compare 37:26, 27). The former betrayer now offered himself. "'Now then, please let your servant remain here as my lord's slave *in place* of the boy, and let the boy return with his brothers. How can I go back to my father if the boy is not with me? No! Do not let me see the misery that would come upon my father'" (verses 33, 34).

It was enough for Joseph. He had sufficient evidence of a radical transformation in the hearts of his brothers. The cruel and heartless Judah of years ago now would surrender his own freedom and remain a servant "'in place of the boy.'"

Centuries later the prophet Isaiah predicted the

love of Another who would *even die* in our place. The prophecy uncannily fulfilled in *the* descendant of Judah, Jesus Christ, reads:

"He was pierced for our transgressions,
        he was crushed for our iniquities;
    the punishment that brought us peace
        was upon him,
        and by his wounds we are healed.
    We all, like sheep, have gone astray,
        each of us has turned to his own way;
    and the Lord has laid on him
        the iniquity of us all" (Isa. 53:5, 6).

No longer could Joseph hide his real identity. Amid loud sobs he exclaimed, " 'I am Joseph!' " (Gen. 45:3). He did not vindictively rail at his brothers or threaten them with punishment, nor did he nurse any grievances. While Joseph had subjected them to a rigorous trial, he cared tenderly for their welfare. In their agitation and distress they had failed to draw the logical inferences from a number of significant incidents. The quiet words of reassurance spoken by Joseph's steward and his remarkable hospitality to them should have raised their suspicions (chap. 43: 23, 24). Similarly, the governor's repeated concern for their father and brother, as well as his display of affection for Benjamin, revealed more than casual interest in their family (verses 7, 27-29). Likewise, the men failed to recognize the import of the prime minister's knowledge of their exact ages even though they were children of four different mothers (chaps. 43:33; 44:12). All of these extraordinary incidents should have aroused their attention to the unusual relationship that existed between them and the governor.

While they had sought to placate the prime minister and win his good will with gifts, they failed to discern that he had already been reaching out to them (chap. 43:13, 24-29). The relation between Joseph and his brothers vividly illustrates many human efforts to attract God's favor. Such attempts do not realize that the Lord's grace and goodness are free and that He anticipates our every appeal. It was the experience of the unknown hymn writer who penned the words:

"I sought the Lord, and afterward I knew,

He moved my soul to seek him, seeking me."

Joseph's concern for Benjamin adds a completely new dimension to the human relationships displayed so far in the book of Genesis. Already we have seen the love of a husband for his wife, depicted in Adam's jubilant response when God presented Eve to him, and in Isaac's affection for Rebekah (chaps. 2:23; 24:67). Similarly, the story of Abraham and Isaac opens our eyes to the love of a father for his son (chap. 22: 1-14). Hagar's care for Ishmael and Rebekah's partiality for Jacob demonstrate a mother's love for her boy (chaps. 21:14-19; 25:28). However, brothers generally demonstrated animosity toward each other. Cain murdered Abel (chap. 4:8, 9); Ishmael cruelly mocked Isaac (chap. 21:8, 9); Jacob and Esau began their sibling rivalry in their mother's womb (chap. 25:22); and his brothers heartlessly sold Joseph to foreign traders (chap. 37:28). Thus the love of a brother for a brother, as exemplified in Joseph's care for Benjamin, is unusual and has been rarely surpassed except in the love of our Elder Brother, Jesus.

As Joseph made himself known to his brothers they "were not able to answer him, because they were terrified at his presence" (chap. 45:3). Their guilt completely immobilized the men. Finally their flimsy pretense had collapsed. Yet Joseph, who had resisted the temptation to ruin another man's home and happiness, assured them; " 'Do not be distressed and do not be angry with yourselves for selling me here, because it was to save lives that God sent me ahead of you. For two years now there has been famine in the land, and for the next five years there will not be plowing and reaping. But God sent me ahead of you to preserve for you a remnant on earth and to save your lives by a great deliverance. So then, it was *not you* who sent me here, *but God*' " (verses 5-8).

Joseph knew that neither chance nor human choice had directed him to his present position. Though he could have become cynical, discouraged, or disillusioned, the young man was convinced that God had led his life through good or ill. In the midst of his brothers' evil scheme to dispose of him another plan was active of which they knew nothing. Joseph shared the convictions expressed centuries later by Paul: "And we know that in all things God works for the good of those who love him, who have been called according to his purpose" (Rom. 8:28).

The prime minister's testimony to his brothers highlights the interplay between God and man, which respects both the freedom of the creatures and the sovereignty of the Creator. God is active in the arena of human affairs, and human works cannot be detached from God's work so as to distinguish completely between the two spheres. While the Lord respects human choices, mankind neither manages its own future nor limits the divine outreach by its decisions. The Lord is at work through, or even against, human deeds and makes use of both the laudable and sordid plans of His creatures. While humanity may hold the Lord's purpose in abeyance, it will not alter it. His goal will ever be final. In aligning God's sovereignty with human freedom, the Bible alerts us that even our best-laid plans are only provisional, and it encourages us to entrust ourselves to Him. We are neither autonomous nor left to despair.

Jacob's sons found it difficult to believe that Joseph accepted them fully and completely. Their fear and mistrust—harbored over the years—surfaced once again when Jacob died some seventeen years later (chap. 50:15-18). The anguish revealed in their pleas for forgiveness indicates how deep-seated their guilt and consciousness of wrong was. They found it more difficult to believe that they had been forgiven than it was for Joseph to forgive. The incident is an example of the enduring power of guilt and fear, which unresolved will rob a person of peace, health, and energy. Such a resolution God freely offers by his grace. He says, "If we confess our sins, he is faithful and just and will forgive us our sins and purify us from all unrighteousness" (1 John 1:9). Confession and repentance of sin, unreserved acceptance of God's pardon offered freely in Jesus Christ, and restitution of wrong still relieve the burdened conscience and result in peace.

With the descent of Jacob and his family into Egypt, God's prophecy to Abraham met its fulfillment (Gen. 46:1-47:12; compare chap. 15:13-16). Though Goshen offered privacy and isolation from the Egyptians and provided a resting place for Israel and his descendants, it never became their home. Jacob's brothers said to Pharaoh, " 'We have come to live here *awhile*. . . . So now, please let your servants settle in Goshen' " (chap. 47:4). God had instructed Jacob, " 'Do not be afraid to go down to Egypt, for I will make you into a great nation there. I will go down to Egypt with you, and I will surely *bring you back* again' " (chap. 46:3, 4). On his deathbed Joseph assured his brothers, " 'God will surely come to your aid and take you up out of this land to the land he promised on oath to Abraham, Isaac and Jacob. . . . God will surely come to your aid'" (chap. 50:24, 25).

In Jacob's family the chosen people began to be formed, but they were in an alien land. The story could not end in Egypt. They were the seed that awaited a fuller and bigger harvest in the Promised Land. The promise of descendants and land was met partially when the children of Israel left Egypt and settled in Canaan. However, the book of Hebrews informs us that the expectations of the patriarchs surpassed anything our sin-marred world could offer. Faith's eye strained to see a global Eden restored, and faith will not go unrewarded. Soon the scenes depicted by the last book of the Bible will come to pass.

ENDNOTES

[1] Derek Kidner, *Genesis*, Tyndale Old Testament Commentaries (Downers Grove, Ill.: Inter-Varsity Press, 1967), p. 9.

[2] William Shakespeare, *Macbeth*, Act V, scene 5, lines 26, 27.

[3] Nahum M. Sarna, *Understanding Genesis* (New York: McGraw-Hill, 1966), p. 17.

[4] See Raymond F. Cottrell, "In the Beginning . . ." *Review and Herald*, June 29, 1967, p. 12.

[5] Sarna, *op. cit.*, p. 21.

[6] See Emil Schürer, *The History of the Jewish People in the Age of Jesus Christ*, new English version revised and edited by G. Vermes, F. Millar and M. Black (Edinburgh: T. & T. Clark, 1979), vol. 2, p. 471.

[7] Claus Westermann, *Creation*, translated by John J. Scullion (Philadelphia: Fortress Press, 1974), p. 65.

[8] Kidner, *op. cit.*, p. 51.

[9] Claus Westermann, *The Genesis Accounts of Creation*, translated by Norman E. Wagner, (Philadelphia: Fortress, 1964), p. 20.

[10] John C. L. Gibson, *Genesis* (Philadelphia: Westminster, 1981), vol. 1, pp. 103, 104.

[11] Compare Westermann, *Creation*, p. 77.

[12] Ellen G. White, *Patriarchs and Prophets* (Mountain View, Calif: Pacific Press, 1958), p. 54.

[13] Kidner, *op. cit.*, p. 69.

[14] White, *op. cit.*, p. 62.

[15] Isidore Epstein, *Judaism* (London: Epworth, 1945), p. 82.

[16] Compare Patrick D. Miller, *Genesis 1-11: Studies in Structure and Theme*, JSOT Suppl. 8 (Sheffield: University of Sheffield, 1978), p. 28.

[17] Kidner, *op. cit.*, p. 74.

[18] Compare Bernhard W. Anderson, "From Analysis to Synthesis: The Interpretation of Genesis 1-11," *Journal of Biblical Literature*, March 1978, p. 32.

[19] Sarna, *op. cit.*, p. 52.

[20] *The Seventh-day Adventist Bible Commentary*, on Gen. 8:14, p. 260.

[21] Gerhard von Rad, *Genesis*, rev. ed. (Philadelphia: Westminster Press, 1974), p. 124.

[22] *The SDA Bible Commentary*, on Gen. 11:1, p. 283.

[23] White, *op. cit.*, p. 87.

[24] Von Rad, *op. cit.*, p. 160.

[25] White, *op. cit.*, pp. 126, 127.

[26] John Bunyan, *The Pilgrim's Progress* (London: Lutterworth

Press, 1961), p. 104.

[27] Walter Brueggemann, *Genesis: A Bible Commentary for Teaching and Preaching* (Atlanta: John Knox Press, 1982), p. 133.

[28] See E. A. Speiser, *Genesis*, Anchor Bible (Garden City: Doubleday & Company, 1964), p. 120.

[29] *Ancient Near Eastern Texts*, 3d edition, p. 220.

[30] Brueggemann, *op. cit.*, p. 161.

[31] Sarna, *op. cit.*, pp. 145, 146.

[32] White, *op. cit.*, p. 147.

[33] *Ibid.*

[34] Brueggemann, *op. cit.*, p. 186.

[35] White, *op. cit.*, p. 180.

[36] *Ibid.*, p. 179.